INNER TREK

A RELUCTANT PILGRIM IN THE HIMALAYAS

MOHAN RANGA RAO

Thank you Mamatha for this Transformative Journey.

This book project has removed my notion that a book was only a writer's endeavor. As a creator, I have received help and guidance through editing and publishing from Allison K Williams and Melanie Gall.

Thank you, Michelle M. Wallace and Anuradha Goyal.

Contents

AUTHOR'S NOTE

I have been on many treks in the Himalayas but have never experienced such a powerful place as Kailash. The curiosity and eagerness of Mamatha's and my friends inspired me to write this book. I have written straight from my heart, trying to keep ego out of the way. Since English is not my mother tongue, be prepared for a few words used for broader meaning where a Western writer might use sharper, more pinpointed language. It is my intention to share my experience candidly, and in this process might come across as crude. Bear with me.

I assumed this tour to be a moderately difficult trek in the Himalayas and a test on my body. My personal limits would struggle with nature's terrain, my own mind, and the altitude. But the week I spent in a place where the greatest of my ancestral Vedic Hindu sages, great intellectuals and spiritual leaders performed rituals, reverberated with the energy of a cosmic waterfall. The path itself became sacred, containing their memory. It is not surprising that one of the visitors collected stones from the Kailash trail, which he arranged around his bathtub so that as he washed his body, he was reminded of Kailash, thereby cleansing his soul.

We Hindus believe that the Brahman manuvers you to a particular destination based on your Karma; the path chooses you. This adventure in a strange land acted like a mirror into my soul, becoming an inner journey and a transformation.

Though the trek around Mount Kailash is deeply personal, its relevance cannot be limited to the Self. I hope to kindle the imaginations of those who will one day embark on this spiritual voyage, unfolding a new layer of meaning for yourselves.

~Mo

CHAPTER 1

A Deathly Beginning

"Do you know what happens on prime properties of vacant land in Bangalore, Mohan Rao?" The voice was soft but sinister. As the man leaned toward me, holding my gaze, I could smell the alcohol on his breath. "One day," he continued, "someone will call the owner's family to inform them of a dead body lying on their property."

Jalli Jagdish straightened and gave me a cold look. I froze, terrified. Trying to maintain a calm facade, I looked over at my lawyer, advocate Hegde. He was studying me from above his spectacles, which had settled on the bridge of his nose.

There are times in our lives when moral fortitude alone is not enough to get through a situation. A death threat from a land mafia don surely tops this list. The fear I felt was so real that for a second I wanted to jump out of the seat and run back to my car.

After taking a moment to gather my wits, I turned to Hegde. He was sitting nonchalantly on his chair with his glasses pushed back and did not appear at all surprised by Jagdish's intimidation.

"Mr. Hegde," I said, trying my best to speak with a clear and steady voice, "please tell me what this is all about."

After a minute of silence, Hegde removed his glasses, looked at me, and started to speak. "Mr. Jagdish bought the one-acre property adjacent to yours. He intends to build apartments and needs your portion for access to the main road."

"Some brokers recently approached me offering three thousand rupees per square foot," I replied. "The area in Utharhally, now called 'Banashankari Sixth Stage,' has become a prime location."

Jagdish had been busy on his phone, but as I spoke, he pocketed it and looked at me.

"What rate can I expect?" I asked him nervously. "I know real estate rates in Mysore but I am not aware of land prices in Bangalore." When nobody responded I continued, my voice hoarse. "Could you give me an indication number?"

"The issue is not the rate, Mr. Mohan," Hegde replied. "The issue is for you to get out of trouble."

Another chill went down my spine and a pit formed in my stomach. My lawyer Hegde was clearly hand-in-glove with mobster Jalli Jagdish.

My story began in 2012, on a scorching summer day in Bangalore. I had scheduled a meeting with my security supervisor, Nanju, to discuss an incident that had occurred a fortnight earlier when the northern part of the brick wall surrounding my 21,000-square-foot property had been razed to the ground.

The vacant lot, which I had bought a decade earlier, was located in the agricultural belt at the outskirts of Bangalore. After receiving governmental approval for change in land use to residential and after the mind-boggling growth of Bangalore as the Silicon Valley of India, the area had increased tenfold in value. My piece of land was even more valuable than the others in the area, because of all the nearby lots, only my property had access to the main road.

"Any idea who demolished the brick wall?" I asked Nanju as we sat together in his office, which was located on a narrow road at Hanumanthanagar on the second floor of a commercial building.

"I heard the culprit behind this illegal encroachment is Jalli Jagdish, one of the land mafia leaders in the area who poses as a businessman dealing in cement and steel."

Following this conversation, I had hired the services of advocate Hegde to get an order to evict Jagdish. To my surprise, instead of arranging the eviction order, Hegde had called to tell me that Jagdish wished to meet me.

As I sat nervously in the meeting, with Jalli Jagdish tapping at his smartphone, I resisted the urge to look at him. Instead, I glanced at Hegde. I was not surprised at my advocate's disloyalty as this had happened several times in the past with other lawyers. But I was shocked that Hegde had been willing to accept a hefty advance from me before changing sides. As I watched Jagdish and Hegde, their orchestrated intimidation became clear: they planned to scare me out of my senses and force me to part with my site at a throwaway price.

"I would be happy to sell my property to you," I said, trying to sound confident. "But you aren't making me an offer. What price do you have in mind?"

Jagdish raised his right hand and mumbled in his gruff voice, "It is a wise decision to sell. Mr. Hegde will call you later with an offer."

"Okay," I muttered. "I will wait for Hegde's call."

I paused, waiting for them to say something more. The men were both silent. I stood, shook their hands, and left the chamber.

Outside, I found my chauffeur Kashi lounging against the car, shirt open in the heat, watching a group of kids play a game of street cricket. He wasn't expecting me and as I approached, he hurriedly buttoned up his shirt and opened the vehicle door. I climbed in the van and instructed him to head back to Mysore.

But before the van had traveled even a few hundred feet, I noticed a familiar figure sitting on a motorbike on the side of the road, helmet in hand.

"Isn't that Nanju, our security supervisor?" I asked Kashi.

Kashi glanced at the figure sitting on the motorbike. He affirmed, "Yes, sir. That is Nanju."

Suddenly all the pieces fell into place. Nanju was involved with Jagdish and Hegde. He had betrayed me. They were all working together. A feeling of defeat and shame enveloped me for having fallen for Nanju's treachery.

It started to drizzle, and, as usual, Kashi refused to clean the windshield unless it was a downpour. As the raindrops spattered against the glass, my emotions from the previous hour boiled over and I yelled at him to switch on the wipers.

This was the first time in my adult life that I had felt powerless. I felt a sense of panic and anger that my self-respect and dignity had been violated.

I called the only person in the whole world that I could truly trust: my wife Mamatha.

I had been married to Mamatha for twenty-four years. Our relationship is excellent by Indian standards, where "keeping the family together" and "making the relationship work by adjusting oneself" is the priority, with "love" taking second place. I had never looked at any other woman. Mamatha is undoubtedly my better half and without her in my life I could never have made it this far.

"Mamatha," I said when she was on the line, "there's a problem regarding our Bangalore property." I tried to sound unruffled and calm.

"What is it, Mona?" she asked in a worried voice. After twenty-four years, Mamatha knew me well enough to discern my state of terror.

"A mobster is threatening me. He wants me to transfer my Utharhally property to him for peanuts. I'll explain everything once I reach home."

"Where are you now?"

"I just came out of Hegde's office. I'm on my way back and I'll be home in three hours." I heaved a sigh of relief, already calmed by Mamatha's voice.

As the car moved along the rain-spattered road I closed my eyes and went into *Yoga Nidra*, instantly relaxing as I turned my concentration inward.

Bangalore was already a large city and appeared to be growing ten times its size every year. With the massive influx of employees and job-seekers, people were desperate to buy land. The real estate market boomed and even vacant lots started attracting the attention of criminals and opportunists. A sect of criminals and thugs had started the 'land mafia,' an underworld gang of ruthless and diabolical land-grabbers who usurped vacant properties.

Their activities were illegal, but police could do little since the land mafia had significant influence with several influential politicians. Going to the police or to a politician would be of no use and I had wasted enough time and money pursuing those avenues. My fifty-four years of life had taught me a lot of things about myself, but the most important thing was that I don't give up. Even when I am pushed into a corner and threatened, I will not just give in.

I am a lover of life. I am humorous and at times can be cocky and insensitive. But I am also extremely determined, self-assured, and confident. As the youngest of nine siblings in a prosperous family, I always saw the world differently. I was the non-conformist, the dreamer, and the rebel. I always aspired to live on my terms, to take that first step onto an unknown road. In my life I had seen victories, successes, money, and all the indulgences that the material world could offer. I had seen defeats and had faced failures. I had experienced grief in its full and unbearable form when at barely nine years old my first daughter Yogita had died from cancer.

Jalli Jagdish's smirk flashed through my mind. I couldn't stem the panic I felt about my family's safety. I had a licensed Beretta 25-caliber pistol at home, but would that be good enough to protect them? My daughter was twenty-one and my son was sixteen. What if Jagdish abducted one of them? What if he ran me over while I was on my morning jog?

I began to wonder, why was I so attached to this experience of existence? I attempted to console myself by recollecting the famous saint singer Purandara Dasa's words, "All that happened has happened for good. All that is happening is happening well. All that will happen will also be for good. Why are you repenting for what you have lost? What have you created that is destroyed? What have you brought with you to lose?"

The ruminations made me tired and I could feel tension in my jaws and forehead. I started my relaxation technique and within minutes fell again into Yoga Nidra. I awoke suddenly at the sound of loud honking from a passing bus. Out the window I saw KR Mills, which meant my house was just twenty minutes away. Before long, Kashi took a right turn onto my street, I thought carefully about what I should say to Mamatha. I decided to tell her the facts. After all, she should know the truth.

The security guard opened my gate and my dog Daisy, a white, fluffy Pomeranian, started barking ecstatically. There was no way I could enter the house without stroking her for at least a full minute and seeing my carefree, happy pet calmed my nerves somewhat.

The teakwood scent of the front door gave me a soothing sense of relief. I removed my shoes and socks and then I threw my laptop bag on the sofa and went into the washroom to toss my socks in the plastic bin of dirty clothes. I entered the bedroom and as I started unbuttoning my shirt, I heaved a sigh of relief.

My wife Mamatha is a beautiful woman. She has fair skin, an oval face, and large hazel eyes. Her black hair is long and shiny with brown highlights. Just looking at her gives me the strength of a thousand elephants. That evening when I came into the bedroom, Mamatha was resting on the bed, watching television. I changed into shorts and as I closed the wardrobe door and turned toward the bed, she switched off the program.

"Mohan," she asked me softly, "could you explain what happened with Hegde? Why did you sound so nervous on the phone?"

I shook my head and raised my shoulders. "I have never been more shaken in my life. Jagdish threatened serious consequences if I did not sell the Bangalore site to him." I was careful to avoid mentioning the specifics of his threat.

"What? What do you mean, Mona?" she asked, her eyes widening. "What exactly did he say?"

I sighed. I could not avoid telling her the truth. "Jagdish strongly implied that a corpse will be lying in my Utharhally property if I do not sell the land to him."

Without a word Mamatha stood, took my hand and dragged me to the *pooja* room, our prayer room.

The *pooja* room is the most special part of our house. It is a small cubicle of about sixty square feet with marble flooring and intricately-carved glass doors. The eastern side of the room contains two hand-carved wooden tables placed on a wide raised marble platform. On the tables, Mamatha had positioned the idols of Lord Ganesh, a Shiva *lingam,* and

Swami Raghavendra. There are four lamps, two on each side of the gods. Mamatha lit the lamps every morning after her bath and on the days when she was menstruating, she asked me to do it for her, ignoring my protests. The *pooja* room is Mamatha's go-to sanctum for any hardship.

In the *pooja* room, Mamatha immediately sat down on the marble floor. I stood next to her with my hands in my pockets. After a moment Mamatha looked up, glared at me and pulled my arm, forcing me to drop to the ground. I sat next to her and formed a lotus position.

"Put aside your self-righteous attitude," Mamatha said, placing her hand on my knee. "Bow before Lord Shiva and pray for a way out of your mess."

I did not believe that praying would help. But I nodded, more out of fear of Mamatha than of the Almighty Lord Shiva. As I sat, surrounded by silence, I sincerely and honestly tried to shed my ego and surrender to some higher intelligence. I waited for illumination to come to my dark mind, but it didn't happen. Instead, a higher force chose my wife, Mamatha, to reveal a solution to my crisis.

"Mohan," Mamatha said, her voice echoing in the room, "Asha Swarup told me that a dip in Manasa Sarovar and a circumambulation of Mount Kailash will ward off all evils from one's life."

Mamatha's friend Asha was considered an expert on rituals and scriptures and Mamatha had tremendous respect for her advice. But I could not fathom how circling around a mountain would edify me and keep away the Jalli Jagdishes of this world.

Mamatha went on, "Why don't you take a vow in front of Lord Shiva to visit Manasa Sarovar and Mount Kailash?"

I considered Mamatha's suggestion. Making a promise to God was one thing, but making a deal with him was another. But Mamatha had such a pleading look on her face that my dogged agnosticism melted away. I nodded, and closing my eyes, said *Gayatri Mantra,* the only prayer I truly believed.

When the prayer was finished, I looked at Mamatha and saw that she had tears in her eyes. "Please start believing in Lord Shiva and seek His help," Mamatha said.

I closed my eyes again and took a vow in front of God that I would fulfill Mamatha's wishes.

"Mark my words, Mohan," Mamatha declared in her calm and confident manner, "your property issues will be resolved very soon."

CHAPTER 2

Patiala Peg

I was certain that Mamatha's implicit faith in Lord Shiva and my vow to visit Kailash Manasa Sarovar were not surefire exit-passes from my Utharhally fiasco. I believed in the wise old adage, "God helps those who help themselves." Although I needed to take some decisive steps to deal with Jalli Jagdish, I decided not to seek assistance from any of my friends from Bangalore and to instead handle the issue myself.

The first thing I needed to do was to get a new lawyer. Since Hegde worked for Jagdish, I could no longer trust him. From my auditor Kumar, I obtained the contact information for Mehta, a very successful lawyer who specialized in land disputes of prime properties in Bangalore. I called Mehta's office the next morning and arranged an appointment with him that evening in Bangalore.

"Don't worry about any encroachment, Mr. Rao," Mehta said after we had settled in his office and I had explained the situation. "Any structure they put up on your property will be yours."

"How long will it take to evict Jagdish?" I asked.

"It depends. Usually it takes a few years, but you can try to get buyers for the property who will handle Jalli Jagdish and settle the dispute. I will spread the word around."

"That would be a big help." I thanked Mehta and signed the papers that legally authorized him to take over my case. That night, I returned to Mysore feeling relieved. I assured Mamatha that the fiasco would soon be over. But deep inside, I was still apprehensive about Jalli Jagdish's threat.

A week later, I received a call from Mehta. "A client of mine, Suresh, has a partner with a lot of political influence. He is interested in buying your Utharhally property. I explained the situation, including Jagdish's involvement. Please expect his call in the next hour."

"Thank you, Mr. Mehta," I said, relieved.

"Please be aware that they will bargain hard," he warned me.

I assured Mehta that I was not concerned about bargaining. I was thrilled that someone was ready to take on Jalli Jagdish. Price was a secondary issue.

Later that afternoon, I received a call from Suresh in Bangalore. "Mr. Rao, we heard from Mr. Mehta that you're selling off your Utharhally property and we're interested in buying it."

"Are you aware that Jalli Jagdish has razed a part of my compound wall and put up an illegal structure at the site?"

"Yes. My uncle is a state minister and we know how to handle the land mafia. In fact, we specialize in dealing with encroached sites."

"Excellent," I replied. "Why don't you come down to Mysore to take this forward?"

"Sure, sir," he said. "Just tell me when." We set a date to meet at a hotel in Mysore the following Monday.

My hometown of Mysore contained many open-air restaurants. Greens, the hotel where I had arranged to meet Suresh and his partner, was located very close to my home. The building had originally been used a movie studio. After the studio closed down, the space was converted into an eco-friendly hotel with an open restaurant and I dined there frequently.

That evening, I arrived promptly at seven. The restaurant was almost empty; of the dozen bamboo tables arranged in the large space only one was occupied. I sat down and a waiter approached. He was wearing a creased white uniform with large black buttons. "How are you, sir?" he asked.

"I'm fine, thanks," I said. I ordered a pint of Kingfisher beer and the waiter quickly brought it over.

As I lifted my mug to take the first sip, two men came to the table. One was short and frail with a friendly face and a relaxed demeanor. He carried a large folder, which I assumed contained copies of my property documents. The other man was tall and appeared more businesslike than his companion. Both men were in their thirties.

I stood up to greet them.

"I am Suresh and this is my partner Manjunath," the shorter man said.

"Hello, Suresh," I said, smiling at his companion and settling back into my bamboo chair. "What will you have?"

"I would like to have vodka." Suresh smiled back at me. "A Patiala peg?"

"And you, Mr Manjunath?" I asked his partner.

"I will have the same."

"Do you know how they measure a Patiala peg?" I asked Suresh.

"No."

"A Patiala peg is measured from top of the index to the base of the little finger when held parallel to one another, against the side of the standard 26.5 oz (750ml) glass bottle. It's a little more than two standard drinks."

I waved to the waiter who hurried over, likely remembering the generous tips I had left during my previous visits. I ordered two Patiala pegs and another pint of beer.

When the beverages were delivered, we drank in silence for several moments. I then asked Suresh, "Have you dealt with land mafia thugs before?"

Both Suresh and Manjunath looked at each other and smiled. Suresh dipped two of his fingertips in his drink. He gently tapped the drops on the table and closed his eyes in an apparent toast to the Almighty. Then he lifted his glass and said, "There is no mafia or underworld that we have not seen. These men are tough only on the exterior. They have their internal demons and fears, just like everyone else."

"Mehta told you about Jagdish's encroachment?" I asked. "How he has occupied my land and has used threats to convince me to sell at an insanely low price?"

"You leave that to us, sir," Manjunath smiled.

"I'm curious," I said to Suresh, "how will you deal with Jagdish?"

"We will make a deal with him. This will be done through my uncle whose favors Jagdish needs for quarry contracts. Besides, even if the property is at Utharhally, which is Jagdish's territory, he often buys land in Arkavathy, which we control. We have a sort of quid pro quo compromise."

"Mr. Mehta confirmed that you have agreed to my asking price of forty-five million rupees," I replied.

"Did Mr. Mehta tell you that in payment, we will be giving you a commercial property in Jayanagar worth thirty million and the balance in deferred payments spread over a year?" Suresh asked.

"Yes. But what is the guarantee that your Jayanagar Property is worth thirty million?"

Suresh removed an envelope from his folder and handed it to me. It was a valuation report from a chartered engineer, assessing his property at thirty million rupees.

"Then it's a deal," I said. I shook hands with both men, feeling ecstatic and relieved.

That night, as I lay with Mamatha in our double bed, I could not keep from smiling. "Mamatha, Jalli Jagdish is out of our lives for good!" I announced.

Mamatha took a moment to reply. "I knew the Utharhally issue would be solved the minute you vowed to visit Kailash Manasa Sarovar," she said.

"You and your magical thinking," I swore under my breath.

The next day, Mamatha suggested that we donate a percentage of the sale proceeds to a holy cause. That seemed a lot easier than visiting some faraway mountain, so I quickly responded, "Absolutely, Mamatha. Thanks for reminding me."

The next week a group of poor street cleaners approached me for a donation to help build a Maramma temple in their neighborhood. After some discussion, Mamatha and I decided to fund the entire project. Construction began in late 2014 and by early December 2015, the temple was ready to be opened. The estimated construction cost of $40,000 USD had escalated to $90,000 USD, but I was determined to build something to be proud of. As a gesture of thanks, the president of the local community association had arranged for my mother and father's names to be engraved on the temple gate. The finished building was beautiful and was the talk of the surrounding suburb.

Once the temple was complete, I felt that I had at least partially repaid the vow I had made to Lord Shiva in the *pooja* room. Mamatha didn't agree.

"But Mamatha," I protested. "I have fulfilled all my promises to you."

"The vow was not to me, Mona, it was to the Almighty. And it is not yet fulfilled. We haven't yet visited Manasa Sarovar and Mount Kailash."

I sighed within me. To my mind, I had surely pleased the gods through the construction of this beautiful temple.

Mamatha started mentioning Kailash Manasa Sarovar almost daily. Whenever she did, I quickly changed the subject. But I suspected she would never let it drop entirely.

CHAPTER 3

The Holy Man

It was a beautiful sunny morning in April, 2016. I tossed my tennis racket onto my bag and collapsed on the wooden bench by the court. It was only 8:00 a.m., but the air was already sweltering and humid. Our tennis court was blessed with plenty of large trees all around and my mornings were filled with the cheerful sounds of birds chirping and cranes whooping, which helped me relax after the strenuous games.

I was feeling good. My daily tennis matches had kept me in sound health for over two decades and this particular morning I had played four sets, winning two of them with the help of my talented younger playing partner, Varun.

I picked up my racket and was inspecting the condition of the grip when I caught a glimpse of someone approaching me. It was Nagraj, the real estate broker who handled all my property transactions. The previous week, Nagraj had sought my financial assistance in supporting religious rituals at Rama Mandir, a temple near his house that had a fire altar for *Vedic* rituals. I had asked him to meet me at the tennis court this morning to discuss the matter.

Accompanying him was a tall, pious-looking man, clad in a white *dhoti* and shirt. He had the untrimmed gray beard typical of Hindu priests. From his unglamorous demeanor and the serenity of his countenance, it was apparent that he was a scholar.

"*Namaskarasaar saar*," Nagraj said. "This is Shastri Galu, a Sanskrit scholar and an expert on Vedic rituals."

"*Namaste*," the pious-looking man greeted me.

Nagraj continued, "I told you about the different *homas*, the Vedic fire rituals. Shastri Galu wished to explain them further."

Shastri began, "Each year, we conduct several homas that involve sacrifices to the fire element, Agni, and unique offerings are cast into the flames while chanting Sanskrit Vedic hymns. Vibrations created by the homas have a profound effect on the atmosphere and surroundings since they are performed with the intention of universal happiness and peace. Fire is the element associated with the upward motion of divine energy and is considered to be the most powerfully-purifying element.

"How do these rituals benefit society?" I asked Shastri.

"The Vedas say that a sacred fire ritual along with Vedic hymns and *yajnas,* sacrifices, will promote and protect higher human values. The ritual benefits everyone participating at physical, psychological, and spiritual levels. The spiritual significance of homa is to raise the general level of human consciousness. People who attend our annual yajnas report their lives are much improved."

As Shastri spoke, his solemnity and reverence made me ponder my own faith. I always faced a dilemma when it came to my identity as a Hindu Brahmin. For me, to be religious conveyed a connotation of the fear of God and the feeling that one must attend worship services to avoid being sent to Hell. In contrast, spirituality had positive connotations of inner contemplation and self-discovery. While I detested the archaic rituals and hierarchical caste system of Hinduism, I had immense reverence for the spiritual and intellectual sophistication of the Upanishads. The mature state of consciousness and awareness advocated in Vedanta was truly an enlightening revelation to me.

Shastri removed a colorful leaflet from the cotton bag that hung from his shoulder and passed it to me. The booklet contained a long list of different rituals, mostly homas, with the first one indicating a cost of $3,000 USD. I was surprised to see such a large amount.

"Sir, the first two events have already been taken," he said. I followed Shastri's forefinger as he pointed to the third homa in the list. "This one is not yet taken by anybody."

"Rudra Homa," it read, and indicated an amount of $500 USD. This was the same mantra that Mamatha had been urging me to listen to on YouTube ever since the temple opened.

"I'll take it," I said. "I will send the check through Nagraj." I pointed out the item on the list and asked, "Shouldn't it be called 'yajna' instead of 'homa' like in the Vedas?"

Shastri smiled. "Homa is one of the activities in a yajna. Homa refers to the procedure of putting your sacrificial oblations into the fire." He paused briefly and said, somewhat hesitantly, "Sir, if you don't mind my saying, it is more important that you participate in the rituals than merely donate the money to fund them."

I was not at all interested in sitting for hours in front of the fire listening to Vedic hymns. However, I did not wish to hurt Shastri's feelings. I said, "Let me know the date and I will come with my wife."

I rose from the bench and shook Shastri's hand while moving my head sideways in the customary Indian manner which conveyed, "Okay. We are done." I offered Shastri back his leaflet.

"Please, keep the leaflet. It is for you." Shastri brought his hands together and dipped his head in a slight bow.

In response, I brought my two hands together and said, "*Namaskara*."

My offer to sponsor Rudra Homa was more to please Mamatha than to try to uplift the welfare of humanity. Mamatha was far more religious than I and she never missed her morning prayers and her chants of Vedic *shlokas*, particularly Lalita Sahasranama. Most of my fights with Mamatha had been over my reluctance to accompany her on visits to temples and pilgrimages.

If there was one thing I hated, it was carrying out rituals advised by an astrologer or a priest. When my first daughter was born blind, I wasted time and money on a plethora of religious ceremonies and rituals in an attempt to restore her vision. However, she never gained her sight and I had given up listening to seers and shamans. Mamatha, however, still had great reverence for miraculous solutions.

On the day of the ceremony, the Rudra Homa procedure began by inviting the gods and offering prayers. Shastri sacrificed my offerings and oblations, which consisted of ghee, milk, curd, sugar, saffron, grains, coconut, scented water, incense, seeds, petals, and herbs. As he cast them into the fire, hymns were sung to the sounds of *svaha*.

At around 1:30 p.m. the collective chanting reached a crescendo, marking the conclusion of the homa. At that time, Shastri beckoned to me with his head and I went to stand beside him. Two men came toward us carrying a seven-foot wooden spatula, which they handed to me and another man. The Vedic hymns became louder and louder as the group raised their voices. Shastri poured out the last remaining portion of ghee, signaling the final part of the ritual, *Poornaahuti*.

Mamatha watched in awe as Shastri poured enough ghee to serve the entire Jayanagar suburb for a day through the spatula's carved-out opening. The *homakunadam*, the flames in the altar, touched the ceiling. After the chanting ended, Shastri collected the ash from the charred offerings.

The ash from the ritual fire was considered holy and was believed to act as a repository of healing energy. As per our sacred tradition, I used my ring finger to put a *Tilak* on Mamatha's forehead by bringing my right arm around her right side. I then applied the holy ash on my forehead while I watched Mamatha, who appeared blissful and content.

Mamatha is a big fan of rituals. I, on the other hand, usually carry out the oblations fretting and fuming. But this ritual triggered a spark of contemplation and new inner energy in me, mainly from the reverberations of the collective Vedic chanting. The act of sacrificing those materials and watching them consumed by the flames made me feel like the negativities in my life were being burned away.

"You know what Asha said when I told her about our Rudra Homa?" Mamatha asked from the passenger seat after the ritual had ended and we were driving back home.

"What?" I drove carefully, keeping my eyes on the narrow street.

"She wanted to know when we're visiting Mount Kailash and Manasa Sarovar." The bell from the temple near our home chimed loudly, serenading our conversation. "I feel that we should both do the Kailash Manasa Sarovar trek before the end of the year."

"Why do they call it Kailash Manasa Sarovar?" I asked, hoping to sound interested.

"Mount Kailash is near the holy Manasa Sarovar Lake and pilgrims visit both places," Mamatha explained. She went on to say that the tour involved a thirty-mile trek around Mount Kailash at an altitude of over 18,000 feet.

In the past several years, Mamatha and I had completed more than thirty hikes in the Western and the Eastern Ghats of South India, including Mullayangiri, the tallest peak in Karnataka, and a half-day trek in the Malana peak near

Kasolat, 8,100 feet in the Himalayas. But I was unfamiliar with Mount Kailash.

Later that week, as I was eating breakfast, Mamatha mentioned the topic again. "I learned that Kailash Manasa Sarovar is only allowed between April and August each year," she said, "and that only a limited number of pilgrims are allowed on the trek."

"Oh?" I nodded, taking a bite of my *paratha*.

"I tried to find out who organizes trips to Mount Kailash," she said, carefully arranging cutlery while deliberately avoiding my gaze. "I called several local travel agents but no one knew how to get there."

I have always loved traveling. Travel for me is mental transportation, not merely physical. It creates a space that takes me far away from mundane and banal thoughts. I learn from the scenes, the people, the local cuisine, the airports, the streets, and, of course, the nightlife.

As I approached sixty, I started to gravitate more toward trekking and adventure travel with a focus on exploring mountain ranges. Hiking and trekking had become a meditative regimen for me. Mountains gave me a sense of the wonder of creative intelligence, secluding me from the rest of the world and sharpening my power of observation: a flower seducing an insect, a squirrel leaping about on the branches of a tree, a bird flying past. None of it escaped my attention. And, in addition to new experiences, traveling put me in touch with new people from around the world.

But this trip didn't seem like the sort of adventure I would enjoy. To me, an organized tour—especially one which was also a pilgrimage—was not something I would cherish. I knew about the Holy Lake of Manasa Sarovar (also called Mana Sarovar), as well as about Mount Kailash. I had read hundreds of books on our religion and history and considered myself a well-informed man. I knew that Mount Kailash was in the Himalayas, but not its exact location.

"Where is Kailash?" I asked, getting up with my plate in my hand. I almost dropped the plate in astonishment when I heard Mamatha's response.

"Mount Kailash is in Tibet."

CHAPTER 4

To a Mountain

"Tibet?" I asked in surprise, trying to picture the location in my mind. "How can such an ancient and important Hindu pilgrimage and the abode of Lord Shiva end up in China?"

"Who knows? Ask Lord Shiva," Mamatha replied.

"No wonder you're not getting anywhere with local travel agents. My brother Krishna did that pilgrimage before. I'll check with him how he got there."

At my office the next day, I did some research about Mount Kailash. I was astonished to learn that it was not only revered by Hindus, but also by Tibetan Buddhists, Jains and followers of the Bon religion. "*Kora*" is the Tibetan equivalent word for the Hindu "*parikrama*" which means circumambulation or revolution. Just like the Hindus, Tibetans believe that walking the thirty-mile circumference of Mount Kailash at an elevation of 16,000-18,000 feet will absolve them of sin and bring about enlightenment.

My brother Krishna and I share an office, and I asked him about his trip. "Krishna, you have been to Kailash Manasa Sarovar, no? Who organized your trek?"

Krishna cocked his head. "Oh my God, what a beautiful place. And I'm the only one in our entire family who has been there." Krishna proudly reiterated his unique status as the only 'Kailash return' in our extended family of sixty-eight relatives.

"How did you go?" I asked.

"Suma and I went through a travel agency called Atmadarshan," Krishna replied. "We started in Katmandu and traveled in Land Cruisers with twenty-five trekkers and six Sherpas. We drove for three days to reach Lake Manasa Sarovar."

"Three days!"

"Yup. It was so dusty that we had to stop and clear the windshield every hour. The wipers were useless. We stayed one night in Shigatse and the other in Saga.

"Did you do Parikrama of Mount Kailash?"

"No," Krishna admitted. "Unfortunately, I didn't visit Mount Kailash. I had just had a cold and became short of breath after I took a dip in Lake Manasa Sarovar. My Sherpa guide had to run to a lower altitude with me on his back and rub my chest and administer oxygen until I could breathe normally. One of the Sherpas in our group, a seventeen-year-old, actually died from the altitude. We all watched helplessly as the other Sherpas gave him oxygen and tried to help him breathe. I didn't want to risk my life after the scare in the lake. And besides, we were told there was a heavy snowfall around the mountain paths. The closest I got to Mount Kailash was viewing it from the banks of the Holy Lake."

"That's too bad," I said, seeing how regretful Krishna appeared.

"I saw it from a distance. But I'm going back next year."

I explained to Krishna that I, too, planned to make the pilgrimage.

"Not many agents organize Kailash Manasa Sarovar tours. How will you get there?" he asked. "We went nine years ago but I no longer have the details of the agent."

"That's all right," I replied. "Mamatha is searching on the Internet. She hopes to find a travel agency that specializes in arranging trips to Tibet."

That evening I was lying on my bed watching television when I heard Mamatha arrive home from a wedding reception. I kept watching the cricket game as Mamatha shut the front door and entered our room. She was dressed in a yellow silk sari with a matching yellow blouse and looked stunning.

"Mohan, guess what?" Mamatha tossed her purse on the bed. "Asha congratulated us on successfully carrying out the Rudra Homa ritual."

"Speaking of rituals," I said, "Krishna and Suma only went up to Lake Manasa Sarovar and returned without going to Mount Kailash. It seems Krishna had trouble breathing and had to be carried down on the back of a Sherpa."

Mamatha changed into her house dress and sat next to me. She took out a pair of earphones and plugged them into her smartphone. She said, "Mohan, please listen to this. The kind of positive energy that the Vedic hymns create is incredible."

I put the buds in my ears, occasionally stealing a glimpse at the cricket score on television. Reluctantly, I forced myself to listen to a group of Hindu Brahmin priests chanting hymns. At first, the chanting brought up childhood memories of temple rituals, but soon I started feeling a current flowing from the crown of my head. Within minutes, I was elevated into a different dimension of focused attention and I was quite surprised by the calming effect that collective Vedic chanting had on my psyche. It resonated within me and I had a strange sensation, like when you listen to your favorite childhood song years later.

"We should do it, Mona," Mamatha reiterated once I took out the earbuds.

"Do what?"

"We should go to Kailash."

Deep inside, I was still hesitant to take the trip. I hoped I would be able to find another way of fulfilling my vow without going all the way to Tibet. But I knew better than to argue with Mamatha once her mind was made up, especially as I had given my word to the Almighty in her presence.

I restrained myself from telling Mamatha about the young Sherpa who had died while accompanying my brother's group, hoping that Krishna's breathing issues were enough to make Mamatha drop the idea of this pilgrimage. It wasn't the risk that bothered me; I loved the Himalayas and I was not at all concerned about the dangers of high altitude. It was just that I always disliked pilgrimmages and the noise and litter around famous Hindu places of worship. There seemed to be a connection between the pious prayers of Hindu pilgrims and the trash they left behind. Also, I was not looking forward to traveling in a group with a bunch of frail, pious-looking pilgrims.

A fortnight passed without any developments, and I was secretly happy that this *Kailash Yatra*, this religious journey, appeared to be a thing for the distant future. I hid my inner pleasure well. But Mamatha's resolve to visit Lord Rudra's abode did not wane.

Mamatha started listening to Vedic chants of Rudra while cooking. "You know, Mohan," she said, as she poured out a cup of *dosa* dough on the pan, "just listening to these Vedic chants blesses you with both worldly and spiritual benefits including good health, peace of mind, and pure joy."

A couple of days later, Mamatha forwarded me an email. It was from Shekar Treks, a travel agency based out of Bangalore that ran a ten-day Kailash Manasa Sarovar tour. The next available date was June, 2016. The trip cost $3,000 USD per person and would be personally organized and supervised by the founder of the organization, who, after surviving the attack on the Twin Towers in New York City, had returned to India to dedicate his life to helping devotees undertake the Kailash Yatra pilgrimage.

Tour participants had to pay a deposit and confirmation details would be sent by email after entry permits from the Chinese authorities were obtained. The bottom of the message contained the Shekar Treks bank account details.

I knew that if Mamatha sent me an email with a travel plan for a tour, it meant the decision was already made. My role was to express my delight at her initiative and dutifully transfer the amount. I immediately wired the deposit and sent a copy of the transfer details to Shekar Treks and Mamatha.

"Mohan, do you know the kind of hardships that pilgrims undergo?" Mamatha asked me later as we drank our evening tea. "Many families with meager financial resources spend what for them is a fortune to see Mount Kailash."

I could not help but sneer inside at the blind faith centered on a mountain peak so far away. The most I knew about Tibet was that about fifty miles from my home in Mysore City, Karnataka, there was a settlement of nearly 70,000 Tibetans, mostly monks. They lived on 3,000 acres of land at Bylakuppa, the first of many Tibetan exile settlements in India. Their presence caused considerable political tension, as the Chinese government was unhappy with the Indian government's support of Tibetan Buddhists.

"The climb to the face of Mount Kailash involves ascending to 19,000 feet above sea level," she said.

I had been to Leh in Ladakh at 11,500 feet, where the lack of oxygen gave me a mild headache. Even simple activities like putting on hiking boots had demanded more effort and energy than at normal altitudes.

"Last year, at least ten Indian pilgrims visiting Kailash died in the storms and from high-altitude sickness while carrying out their holy circumambulation around Mount Kailash," she continued.

"Hmmmmm," I said. I wasn't worried. Since the trip to Leh I had become much fitter. Also, I had been on several other treks and had experienced no difficulties.

As the trip quickly became a reality, I decided to find out more about Tibet and Mount Kailash. I already knew that the mountain was held sacred by four faiths: Hinduism, Buddhism, Jainism and Bon. While in Hinduism, Mount Kailash is considered to be the abode of Lord Shiva, Buddhists regard Mount Kailash as an embodiment of Lord Buddha. Jains believe Mount Kailash was the place where Rishabh deva, the first Jain *Tirthankara*, attained Nirvana, the freedom from the cycle of death and rebirth. In Bon, a religion that predates Buddhism in Tibet, Mount Kailash is known as the seat of all spiritual power.

I wanted to know everything I could about the legends the Holy Lake and the Holy Mountain carried. I was interested in the mountain's geology and Lake Manasa Sarovar's almost universal appeal.

Four of the largest Indian rivers: Sutlej, Brahmaputra, Indus, and Karnali (a tributary of the Ganges) had their sources in the vicinity of Mount Kailash. The mountain was a geometrically-critical point and had a unique physical shape, like the pyramids of Egypt, with four nearly-symmetrical sides. Dr. Ernst Muldashev, a Russian ophthalmologist based in Ufa, came up with a theory that Mount Kailash was actually an ancient man-made pyramid that was surrounded by smaller pyramids and linked to pyramids in Giza and Teotihuacan. As he described, "The [mountain's] dividing lines show up clear and distinct which gives the mountain the facade of having been built by giant hands of huge blocks of reddish stones."

Many believed that Mount Kailash was an *axis mundus*, a cosmic axis, and that the earth pivoted on the mountain, much like a magnetic needle rotating in a compass. Others believed that the mountain was connected to mysterious monuments across the globe, including Stonehenge, which was exactly 6,666 kilometers (4166.25 miles) away. One photographer captured a Sanskrit *"Om"* symbol, formed from snow on the face of Kailash.

Although Mount Kailash was a sacred site for billions of people, it was so remote that only a few thousand pilgrims traveled there each year. The journey required trekking at high altitudes under inhospitable conditions, including extreme cold and rugged terrain. The trip could easily prove fatal, as any sudden and hasty ascent to high altitudes could cause life-threatening high-altitude sicknesses.

Many pilgrims described how, after twelve hours on the mountain, their hair and nails grew at a pace equaling two weeks' growth in normal conditions. This immediately caught my interest and the more I read about the mountain, the more my curiosity toward Mount Kailash increased.

For the first time since Mamatha had proposed the Kailash trip, I started to feel intrigued and excited. I wanted to understand the significance of Kailash, to see and experience the scientific mysteries. I was amazed by the courageous struggle of Tibetans to maintain their culture and religious traditions in their land.

His Holiness, the Dalai Lama, wrote in his book, *My Tibet,* "If people are so highly developed spiritually that they can practice their religions effectively by staying in one place, even in some unholy place, then a pilgrimage may not be important for them."

Since I didn't consider myself to be pious and was not religious at home or in temples, perhaps this pilgrimage was exactly what I needed.

CHAPTER 5

Pilgrimage or Peril

After my research about Mount Kailash, I had started to develop an enthusiasm for the trip to Tibet. Three weeks after paying the deposit, Shekar Treks called to inform me that the travel permits had been granted. As the trip became a certainty, I did more reading about mountaineering and trekking in the Himalayas and I learned that the most exciting and incredible aspect of mountain adventures was the support and resilience of the Sherpas.

The word 'Sherpa' evolved from two words: *sher,* which meant east, and *pa,* which meant people. Sherpas come from the eastern regions of Nepal and work on several mountains, transporting essential items into dangerously high altitudes and guiding climbers through challenging terrain.

I learned that circumambulation of Kailash Mountain involved a total walking distance of forty miles. Thankfully, the Chinese had built a road that covered the first ten miles, which left thirty miles to hike on foot. Generally, on the first day, trekkers covered ten miles. The second day was the toughest, with a fourteen-mile trail that reached an altitude of 18,700 feet. The final day was a short and sweet six miles.

Although the distance around Kailash is much shorter than the hike to Everest base camp, it is much tougher due to the altitude. The peak altitude at the Everest base camp is 17,600, over a thousand feet less than the altitude when ascending Kailash's Dolma La pass. Without divulging my worry about the dangers of high altitudes to Mamatha, I decided to keep a very close watch on our fitness levels and find out more about preventing altitude-related sickness.

We soon received our itinerary and learned that the trip would start with a flight to Kathmandu from New Delhi on June 11, 2016. The itinerary read:

June 11:	Arrival in Kathmandu. *Yatra* orientation and tour briefing. Overnight stay in Kathmandu.
June 12:	Optional early morning Everest flight. Visit to Pashupathinath and Jala-Narayana temples. Afternoon flight to Nepalgunj. Yatra Orientation and Tour briefing during dinner, overnight in Nepalgunj.
June 13:	Early morning flight to Simikot. Travel to Hilsa by helicopter. After all group members reach Hilsa, cross the suspension bridge over the Karnali River to enter Tibet and drive to Takalkot. Complete Chinese immigration formalities and overnight stay in Takalkot.

June 14:	Rest at Takalkot (13,200 feet altitude) for acclimatization.
June 15:	Travel by highway from Takalkot to Manasa Sarovar via Rakshastal Lake.Take holy bath near Tru-Gompa, start Manasa Sarovar Parikrama by bus and reach Chiu Gompa. Overnight stay in dormitory rooms; view Divine Lights in Manasa Sarovar.
June 16:	Perform Puja in Manasa Sarovar and proceed to Darchen. Possible evening visit to Astapad. Overnight stay in Darchen.
June 17:	Visit Yama Dwar and offer prayers. Start Parikrama and reach Dirapuk. View north face of Kailash. Overnight stay in Dirapuk.
June 18:	Cross Dolma La pass; have *darshan* of Gowri Kund and reach Zuthulpuk. Overnight stay in Zuthulpuk.
June 19:	Complete Parikrama and reach Darchen. Travel by vehicle and reach Takalkot by noon. Complete China immigration and proceed to Hilsa. Travel by helicopter to Simikot and overnight stay at Simikot.
June 20:	Early morning flight to Nepalgunj. Proceed to Lucknow by bus. Overnight stay at Lucknow.
June 21:	Return flight to Bangalore.

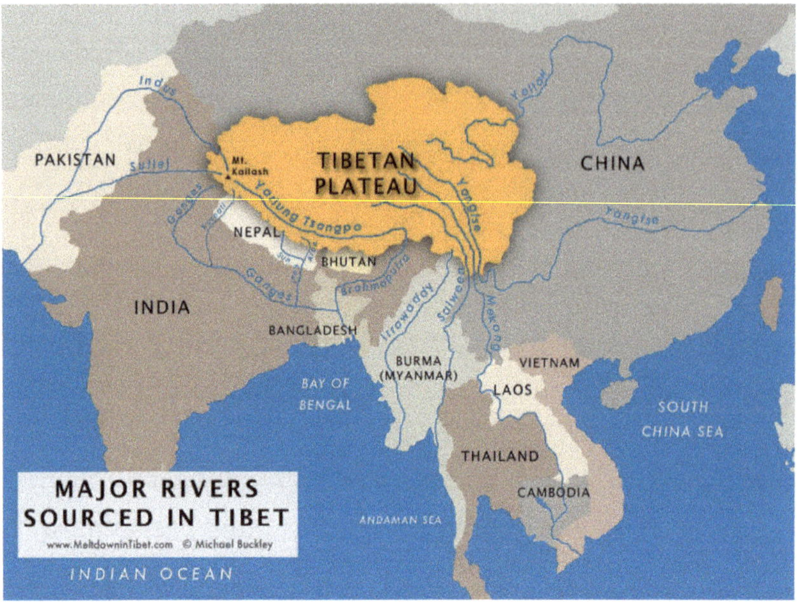

As usual, Mamatha started to prepare for the trek right away, ordering gloves, thermal socks and other items. The only physical contribution I made in preparing for the trip was the purchase of two trekking sticks through Amazon that we later had to throw away due to their clumsy opening mechanisms. Mamatha was wonderful and got everything we needed, meticulously organizing all our supplies. She even obtained a medical certificate with her hemoglobin level, which was at a healthy 12. Mine had been tested two years before and was 15.4. The amount of hemoglobin in the blood determined the amount of oxygen which needed to be carried along and it played a critical role at high altitudes where the air was thin.

"Mona, have you started packing yet?" she asked one night, as I sat on our bed watching television.

I was more of a last-minute packer. "We still have more than a week."

Mamatha sighed. She had been to Kedarkantha peak in the Himalayas at 12,500 feet, about sixty-five percent of the altitude of Kailash, and she considered herself an expert in encountering snow-clad mountains and high altitudes.

"Are you even aware what you're up against on a 18,000-foot trek in the Himalayas?" she asked.

"I can manage," I casually replied.

We had both done a Himalayan trek near Kasol the previous December at an altitude of around 8,000 feet.

"Mamatha, remember how fast I was during the Manali trek? Even our guide Manoj couldn't keep up with me," I gloated. "I wasn't the least bit affected at the altitude there and I'm sure I'll be fine at Kailash."

Mamatha was used to my boasting, and I was used to following her advice, as she was usually right. The next day I went to Woodlands Outlet and bought a thick dark brown coat with a woolen collar and hood and proudly showed it to Mamatha when I got home.

"Mohan, did you go through the PowerPoint presentation sent by Shekar Treks?" Mamatha asked during breakfast the next day.

With some difficulty, I swallowed the last bite of my sandwich and lied, "Of course." I had not even opened the message.

"Can you tell me a few pointers about our trek?"

"The main thing is keeping ourselves warm," I began, confident Mamatha would show off her knowledge before I even completed my sentence.

I had guessed right. Mamatha broke in with, "We have to take our craps in open areas for two or three days during the trip."

I immediately asked if she had bought enough wet wipes.

"I have two whole boxes," she assured me. "That's more than enough."

"Please, buy one more box," I begged.

"Go get it yourself if you don't trust me." Mamatha sighed and continued, "We have to sleep in dormitories after Nepalgunj."

Thoughts of burps, farts, and closed doors and windows flashed through my mind. I rubbed my nose.

Mamatha went on, "Alcohol is not permitted during the tour."

"What?" At that moment I almost canceled the tour. "No way, but why?" I almost cried.

"Are you mad, Mona?" Mamatha asked me incredulously. "How can you drink while trekking at high altitudes? It's really dangerous. Can't you live without alcohol for a week?"

I could, but I didn't want to. After all, as far as I was concerned, this was a vacation as well as an adventure. I pictured my hip flasks and vodka bottles and wondered how many I could hide in my duffle bag. But the thought of

Mamatha's disapproval was scarier to me than the risk of high-altitude trekking and I quickly dropped the idea.

By the fourth of June, with our trip still a couple of days away, Mamatha's backpack and duffle bag were packed and bulging while mine lay empty in a corner. Mamatha had packed all her essentials: warm clothes, Rudra Homa ritual materials and even Hindu holy apparel for me, including a colored dhoti and a shawl which I was sure as Lord Shiva in Kailash that I would never get to wear.

"Won't it be cold out there?" I had objected, when I saw the dhoti. "When will I get to wear this?"

Mamatha didn't answer. The dhoti, a silent weapon of her passive aggression, stayed packed. Also, the 'essentials' that Mamatha stocked did not include *my* essentials: enough alcoholic beverages for two weeks.

"Mona, have you packed your trekking shoes?" Mamatha asked one afternoon, as she pushed her heavy footwear into her bag.

Our two children, Rachita and Rahul, were visiting for the day. My daughter Rachita, who was twenty-five, lived in Bangalore and worked as a PR specialist for Plantronics, an American Company. She was pretty, with a light brown complexion, and was extremely bubbly and energetic. She was a Bharatnatyam dancer and, like me, was into yoga and meditation. In addition to my love of yoga, she inherited my sense of stubbornness and independence. For example, whenever I pestered her for a grandchild, she just smiled and said, "Get a pet."

My son Rahul, who was twenty, worked as an Electronics Engineer for MuSigma, an Indian data analytics company.

He shared my love for tennis and adventure and hoped one day to move to America. Although he was not into yoga or meditation, we often spent time together bonding, drinking together in my "private bar"—my man cave.

When they heard that Mamantha and I were undertaking the Mount Kailash trek, our children had very different reactions. Rachita had no idea about high-altitude trekking and merely asked us to "take care." However, Rahul had done some trekking in the Himalayas, including the difficult Tapovan trek, and I respected any travel advice he had to offer. After Rachita returned to Bangalore, Rahul remained with us as Mamatha and I continued with our packing. There was only space in the bag for one extra set of footwear and I considered the options. I had purchased new, expensive Quechua brand hiking shoes for our treks in the Western Ghats. However, the shoes were very heavy and I felt that at a high altitude they would be more of a handicap than a help while climbing.

"Yes," I answered Mamatha. "I have my Nike jogging shoes."

Mamatha almost dropped the bag she was holding. "Are you crazy, Mona?" she asked. "If you wear shoes without a good grip, you could fall on an icy path. And walking on fresh snow is even more difficult because your feet sink into the snow with every step."

Rahul chimed in, "Appa, are you out of your mind? It's so obvious you don't know anything about trekking at high altitudes!"

"Okay!" I exclaimed. "I'll bring a pair of trekking shoes."

Rahul looked relieved and offered me his Adidas hiking shoes, which were far lighter and more comfortable than the Quechuas. Mamatha merely smiled and said, "Good."

After she was satisfied that I wasn't going to sneak the Nike jogging shoes into my bag, she continued, "Mohan, I've prepared your favorite *avial* for dinner."

Mamatha had turned into a gourmet chef, preparing three- and four-course meals as a token of appreciation for my newfound enthusiasm for Kailash Manasa Sarovar.

After dinner that night, I went through the PowerPoint presentation from Shekar Treks. The first slide that caught my attention was the one about physical fitness and the need for a medical certificate. I considered myself in very good physical form. I had completed a seven-mile mini-marathon in the famous Kaveri Trail Marathon from Paschimavahini to Visweswariah Canal in under seventy minutes. I had won the first runner-up medal in the veteran group. Not bad for a fifty-eight-year-old! I stayed fit by playing tennis each day and frequently climbing the 1,128 steps of Chamundi Hills. For her physical preparedness, Mamatha attended regular yoga sessions and began to take brisk early morning walks.

The day before we left, Mamatha and I went out to buy some last-minute essentials, including, at my insistence, extra wet wipes. Just as we were about to enter into the house, our neighbor Sudha called out from her garden, "When are you leaving for Kailash Manasa Sarovar, Mamatha?"

"Our flight to New Delhi is in two days," Mamatha called back.

"You're going with Shekar Treks, right?" Sudha asked. "Their arrangements are excellent. Our experience with them was fantastic. But one has to be careful, Mamatha. We completed the Parikrama but a forty-year-old lady from our group died of altitude sickness."

After we entered the house, Mamatha was quiet. After a while, she turned toward me and asked, "Mohan, do you think we're doing the right thing?"

"Don't worry, we will be fine," I said.

Thoughts of the dangers we would face flashed through my mind, but I brushed them aside. Right or wrong, soon we would be leaving for the biggest adventure of our lives.

CHAPTER 6

Airports and Toilets

I had always nurtured a secret desire to see Mount Everest. If I couldn't stand at the summit holding a flag like Sir Edmund Hillary or Tenzing Norgay, at least I wished to see it with my own eyes. I had read that some private flight operators took tourists very close to Mount Everest in small airplanes.

Before we left Mysore, I called Shekar Treks to find out if they could organize the plane ride around Mount Everest for Mamatha and me. "What the hell," I figured. "At least I'll get to see Everest from a plane if I'm going to croak."

"It's a forty-five minute flight up and down to see Everest and will cost about 7,000 rupees each," the Shekar representative said, appearing more concerned about clarifying that the price we paid for the trek did not cover the Everest flight than providing helpful information. She added, "You'll have to buy the ticket directly at the airport in Kathmandu."

I wanted a commitment. “Money is not my issue,” I said. “What I want to know is will I get to see Mount Everest up close from a plane?”

“Sir, don’t worry, I will send word to the local agent. We will not send you on your tour without showing you Everest.”

Finally, June 10, 2016 arrived. The day of our departure.

Mamatha and I left Mysore at 7:00 a.m. and reached Bangalore at 10:00 a.m. We stopped to visit with Mamatha’s father in Banashankari, a suburb in South Bangalore. Mamatha and I spent the day recording a narration of my father-in-law’s life to prepare a biography for future generations. Since his stroke Mamatha’s father could not leave the house and so we ordered food from a nearby Indian restaurant and had dinner at home.

Mamatha asked her dad, “Anna, remember Mohan’s Utharhally site?”

“Yes, I do. Was he able to get the illegal encroachment cleared?”

“Mohan sold off the property, Anna.”

“Good for him!”

“In fact, our trip to Kailash was triggered by his site fiasco. But it has taken two years for us to take the trek.”

“What time is our flight to Kathmandu from Delhi, Mamatha?” I asked, deliberately changing the topic as Jalli Jagdish’s face flashed in my mind.

“It’s six in the morning on the day after tomorrow. Our flight to Delhi is tomorrow evening.”

"Mohan, Kathmandu airport is something like Bangalore's old Kalaspalya Bus Stand," my father-in-law said.

"Is it, really?" I asked, astonished.

"Yes, it is a small airport buzzing with passengers frantically hurrying around in confusion."

We went to bed at 9:00 p.m. and, as usual, Mamatha and I got up at 4:30 a.m. There was a Shiva temple a few hundred yards from my father-in-law's house, located on a small hillock called Dharmagiri. The entire perimeter of the temple premises had been paved to create a 750-meter jogging track, half uphill and half downhill. I decided I would hone up my physical endurance by completing fourteen Parikrama, clockwise rounds, of Lord Shiva on Dharmagiri hill, climbing 1,100 feet over a distance of ten kilometers.

While Mamatha once again checked her luggage, I dutifully set out to complete my physical drill. On my seventh lap, while I was running back down the hill, I tripped, fell and banged my head on a water pump. The thud of my head hitting the metal pipe was so loud that I thought I might die before even leaving for Kailash.

Despite the pain, I got up and unflinchingly finished my quota. Afterward, I sat on a stone bench and performed my twenty-minute breathing routine of *Ujjayi*, *Kapal Batti*, *Naadi Shodhana* and *Brahmari* pranayama, unaware that I had just begun a trip to the abode of the inventor of yoga, Adiyogi Lord Shiva.

Prema from Shekar Treks phoned at exactly ten in the morning. She informed us that we would need to pay $1,500 USD to Govind, the guide for the Kailash trek, for "incidental expenses" incurred while obtaining the Chinese visas.

"There goes three thousand dollars to the agents' pockets," I quipped to Mamatha.

"You think so?"

"I don't think so, I know so," I responded, sure that group visas were not actually that expensive.

The flight from Bangalore to Delhi left at 11:20 p.m. We arrived at the airport by 7:30 p.m. and were at the departure gate by 8:00 p.m. I decided to take advantage of the bar across from our departure gate and I drank all the beer my stomach could accommodate.

The new Indira Gandhi International airport in New Delhi was very impressive. As we walked through the terminal, I asked Mamatha, "Would you have imagined twenty years ago that we would have an airport of this caliber in India?"

The flight to Kathmandu was at 6:30 a.m. and we had a long night ahead. The 1970s Bollywood music playing at the airport felt quaint and nostalgic. We bought omega-3 supplements, chose the most comfortable-looking and quietest seats at the airport, and went to sleep.

The plane to Kathmandu was small, with a capacity of about sixty, and our flight was enjoyable. Mid-flight, Mamatha nudged me awake and said, "Pull up your window, Mona."

I was speechless as I gazed at the neverending Himalayan range from my window. As I enjoyed the spectacular view, the blinding sun pierced through the clouds. I reluctantly shut the window so as not to disturb the other passengers. I closed my eyes and imagined Everest, shining in the distance.

When we landed, I was retrieving our bags from the overhead bins when Mamatha tapped on my shoulder. "Mohan, meet Mr. Neelakanta. He's coming along with us."

I put down our backpacks and turned toward a man in his early thirties with a ponytail, a large Tilak and an unshaven face. Kanta looked more like a tantric than a techie.

"Hello," I said, shaking his hand. "First time?"

"No. I have lost count. Fourteenth, I think."

Passengers started moving toward the door of the plane, forcing me to end my conversation. I picked up our backpacks and started toward the exit.

"When did you meet him?" I whispered into Mamatha's ear as we walked along the aisle.

"When you had your hour-long toilet visit at the airport in Delhi," she said.

At Tribhuvan International Airport, we bounced between counters with the other tourists, all of us equally confused at the different immigration forms we needed to fill out and too embarrassed to ask for help. I remembered my father-in-law's spot-on comparison of Kathmandu airport with the oldest bus stand in Bangalore and smiled.

Finally, after finding and filling out the proper forms, Mamatha and I headed outside the airport to the hotel shuttle. The drive to the hotel took only a few minutes. Throughout the short trip, my mind raced with thoughts of the upcoming Mount Everest flight. It would be the fulfillment of one of my life's ambitions, and I could not wait.

CHAPTER 7

Top of the World- Literally

I was surprised by the warm weather in Kathmandu, as well as by the smell of pollution in the air. Since our stay here was only for a day, the very first thing I wanted to do was to arrange the Everest flight. I decided to book the flight right after I checked in to the hotel.

With Hindus making up over ninety-five percent of the population in Nepal, Kathmandu is a city full of temples. I wondered about the condition of these temples since a deadly earthquake had occurred just a year earlier. The worst earthquake in eighty-one years, it had killed over 9,000 people and destroyed over 600,000 homes.

I turned my attention to the interior of the minibus that was taking us to the hotel. Looking around the car, I saw a rolled-up Nepali bill placed in the right armpit of the small bronze statue of the God Ganesh that had been fixed on the dashboard. I asked the driver if the bill was a lucky charm for him and he just smiled without replying.

Hotel Amadablam was clean and relatively new. The front desk was quite large and a young man in a dark suit welcomed us as we arrived.

"What peak is that?" I asked him, pointing to the large photograph of a mountain behind his desk.

"That is Ama Dablam, our holy mountain," he replied.

"What do you mean by 'holy mountain'?" I asked.

Without appearing irritated, he explained, "You see, we Nepalis worship many great Himalayan mountains as gods. The Sherpas call Mount Everest 'Chomolungma' and worship it as the mother of the world. Mount Makalu is worshiped as the deity Shankar, Shiva, by a few communities. Each clan recognizes mountain gods identified with certain peaks they consider their protective deities."

The man handed me our room keys. "Your room number is 708, on the seventh floor. I will send up your suitcases."

As usual, I took the stairs and Mamatha chose the elevator. The room was clean and well-maintained with a view of the surrounding township. It contained two chairs facing the window with a small stool. The king-sized bed had a sheet with a heavy floral design. The large pillows were a little hard and just right for me.

"Do they have room service?" Mamatha asked as she collapsed on the bed and threw her backpack on the floor.

"I don't think so," I said, dropping into one of the chairs and adjusting my watch. It was 10:30 a.m., half an hour ahead of New Delhi.

After a short nap, Mamatha and I decided to visit the famous Pashupatinath Temple, the most sacred Hindu temple of Nepal, which was right across from our hotel. It had been damaged in the earthquake and several parts of the temple were being reconstructed.

The temple complex, sprawling across an acre and a half of land, was one of the seven monument groups in UNESCO's designation of Kathmandu Valley as a cultural heritage site and the oldest Hindu temple in Kathmandu, dating back to 400 C.E. Hindu cremation ceremonies were performed at Pashupatinath Temple at an industrial scale. For Hindus, death is an integral part of the journey of life. They do not believe in bodily resurrection and the reunification of each soul with its physical body, so, unlike in Judaism, Christianity, and Islam, they place no importance on preserving the corpse.

I was used to temples that had a single tall structure, usually pyramidal, that was housed in the middle of a vast rectangular complex. Even from a distance, Pashupatinath Temple appeared very different. The main temple of Pashupatinath was a building with a bunk roof and a golden spire. It was a large rectangle with four main doors all covered with silver sheets. Devotees entering from the western gate would encounter the colossal form of Nandi, Lord Shiva's mythological bull. The Pashupati form of Shivalingum at this holy shrine was about 3.5 feet or 1 meter high.

After we finished our visit, Mamatha and I walked around the temple's outer complex. Toward the eastern corner, we saw a large group of people gathered on the main street watching something on a large platform constructed on the riverbank. We approached the platform and were met with the chilling sight of several corpses being cremated.

"Let's get the hell out of here," I said. I turned to leave, practically dragging Mamatha away.

There were many shops situated on both sides of the road leading to the temple and we stopped in one of them to buy our *rudraksha* beads. Devotees most often wore the prayer beads for protection and while chanting the *Om Nama Shivaya* mantra.

Rudraksha beads are constructed from seeds of the large evergreen trees that grow in the Himalayas. These seeds are associated with Lord Shiva and the rudraksha seeds from Nepal are considered the best since they are perfectly round and extremely strong. They are valued similarly to semi-precious stones. Different meanings and potencies were attributed to seeds with varying numbers of sides and rare or unique beads were valuable and highly prized.

According to details found in the Shivpurana, ancient Indian tomes of literature, there are fourteen kinds of rudraksha. Rudraksha seeds were categorized by the number of faces, or *mukhi*, they contained. Mukhi were deep lines found on the surface of the rudraksha. Scriptures narrated the properties of one to twenty-one mukhi rudraksha and it was believed that in ancient times beads were available from 1-108 mukhi.

Sadhus believed that if a rudraksha was held above drinkable water, it would move clockwise. If the water was poisoned, it would swing anticlockwise. This was also a way of checking the quality of food. If the bead was held above a *pranic* substance, it would move clockwise. If it detected harmful pranic material, it would swing in an anticlockwise direction. I was very keen to try the rudraksha beads on my single malt to see which way they would swing.

Tirupathi, one of the shops, had different semi-precious stones displayed along with several kinds of rudraksha beads. The many salesmen were eager to fill up our shopping cart and it was more than a bit chaotic.

"Could you show me a seven-faced bead for immersion in Lake Manasa Sarovar for my husband?" Mamatha asked the tall salesman behind the counter.

"Madam," he replied, "the more faces on the bead, the more expensive they get. For instance, I can give you one with eleven faces but it will cost you about five thousand Nepali rupees."

Mamatha opened her purse and took out her credit card. "I'll buy one of those and a pair of five-faced ones," she said without flinching.

I was astonished at my wife's quick decision. But as Mamatha later explained, she had implicit faith that if these tree seeds were immersed in Lake Manasa Sarovar before I wore them, they would accumulate positive energy from the environment and spread it throughout my body. It was for this reason that she did not bargain as much as usual.

"Mohan, why don't you also buy a pair of five-faced rudraksha and a small one with eleven faces?" she asked. "You can immerse them in Manasa Sarovar and attach them to your gold chain."

"What about the ones you bought just now?"

"They are for our pooja room at home."

"Well, I don't like buying five- or seven-faced rudraksha from two-faced stores," I said. Mamatha's silent glare instantly erased my smirk.

I obediently picked up two large five-faced rudraksha. There were no eleven-faced beads of the correct size, so instead I chose two small seven-faced beads.

After we shopped, Mamatha and I returned to the hotel for lunch. The large dining hall contained about twelve tables. Lunch was a North Indian buffet, with the items laid out on three separate tables. The first contained salads and vegetarian dishes, the second held three meat dishes, and the third displayed desserts.

I ordered a Nepalese beer called Everest and looked around. A confident-looking woman and a bespectacled, gentle-looking tall man sat at the table behind us. Their faces were almost mirror images. Between her soup helpings, Mamatha whispered to me that they were siblings and were from our group. Their names were Dinakar and Rajasri and they ended up becoming our close friends.

Lunch was passable. I tried the chicken *biryani* and found it needed more spice. Mamatha stuck to her soup and salads.

"Are you our tour guide?" I asked the middle-aged man with the golf cap who had escorted us to the temple and who helped organize the buffet.

He shook his head. "No, I am not. Mr. Shashi is your tour guide. He will join us soon." As I returned to my table, the man added, "By the way, please be ready by four-thirty to visit another temple."

"Which temple?" I asked.

He reverentially replied, "Narayanthan Temple. It's just a few miles from our hotel."

Narayanthan Temple may have only been a few miles away, but the rickety bus that took about an hour to get there was also practically a historic monument.

Jal Narayan is an open-air temple belonging to Lord Vishnu. It lies below Shivapuri Hill, eight kilometers north of Kathmandu. Jal Narayan, locally known as Budhanilkantha temple, contained a giant idol of Lord Vishnu reclining on the coils of the serpent Shesha Naga in a pool of water. The idol is a thousand years old and symbolizes Vishnu lying on the cosmic water before the Universe was created. The sixteen-foot sculpture is the largest stone deity in Nepal.

The Jal Narayan deity was the first representation of Lord Vishnu that I had seen with its back wholly submerged in water. The sight of the gigantic sleeping lord, his four hands holding the *shankh, chakra, gada* and *padma* and the peaceful expression on his beautiful chiseled face, was an awe-inspiring sight. I was genuinely fascinated with the symmetry and accuracy of the facial features of the deity. It evoked a sense of piety and reverence. According to one story, a farmer and his wife were plowing their field when they struck a stone figure, causing it to bleed. The figure turned out to be the lost deity of Budhanilkantha, which was recovered and placed in its present position.

For many years, locals had believed that the stone statue was floating in the pool. In 1957, when skeptics publicly questioned these beliefs, limited access to scientific data failed to confirm or refute the claim. A small chip of the figure was found to be low-density silica-based stone, similar to lava rock. Subsequent requests for access to study the statue's physical nature were declined and the floating statue continues to fascinate.

I took out my phone to snap a photograph of the extraordinary image, but Mamatha pinched me, drawing my attention to the placard that read, "Photography is strictly banned for security reasons."

I sheepishly kept my phone inside my pocket, but another Indian was not as respectful. When he tried to take a video, the person in charge of vigilance showered him with water from a two-inch hose. It sure was an excellent tourist repellent. The Indian ran away from the place with a large portion of his posterior thoroughly drenched.

After we visited the sculpture of Lord Vishnu, we returned to the hotel. At the reception desk, I inquired about our flight to Everest and was told that the plane would leave 6:00 a.m. and that a minimum of sixteen passengers were required for the flight to go ahead.

That evening, Mamatha and I sat in our room and waited for confirmation of the flight. By 8 p.m., no one had turned up to collect the airfare and I was starting to get anxious that the flight would be canceled. At last, at 10:30 p.m., the front desk called. Luckily, sixteen people had signed up to take the flight. The agent instructed us to meet at the reception desk by 5:15 a.m. sharp, as the plane had to take off before 6:00 a.m. I was so relieved that as soon as I climbed into bed, I started snoring.

The only English lesson I remembered from my schooldays was about Mount Everest and the first mountaineers to reach its summit. Edmund Hillary and Sherpa Tenzing Norgay made history on May 29, 1953. The photo that Hillary took of Tenzing standing on the peak with his ice-ax in hand was still vivid in my memory. Ever since then, my heart craved a glimpse of the tallest mountain peak in the world. Perhaps it was for that reason that I awoke at 4:30 a.m. sharp the next morning, without even an alarm. I had assumed the front desk would provide a wake-up call since they had booked the flight, and I can only call it a divine miracle or a cosmic intervention that abruptly woke me from the deep sleep brought on by the exhausting day we had just spent.

"Thank God, Mona," Mamatha said as the elevator door closed and we hurried to the lobby. "If you had not gotten up at the right moment, we would have missed the flight."

At the airport, I could feel the excitement of all the waiting passengers. I was just as excited! I felt like a schoolboy and Mamatha smiled at my enthusiasm. "Hold on," she said as the boarding call sounded. "The plane isn't going to leave without us, Mona. You don't have to run."

As I climbed into the Beechcraft 1900D, a nineteen-seat aircraft, I was delighted to see that each person had a window seat. As I took my place, a flight attendant brought around a bundle of tee-shirts that read, "I never climbed Everest. But I touched it with my heart." I bought two.

The plane took off. It broke through a layer of clouds and the mountain peaks, glistening in the morning sun, were immediately visible. Within minutes of take-off, we were in the white landscapes of the mighty Himalayas. As I looked out over the range, stretching for over 1,500 miles, I thought about the vastness of the Himalayas and goosebumps ran up my arms. It was surreal.

The Himalayas are the highest mountains in the world. Formed during the continental drift when India collided with

Asia, the Himalayas rose along the line of impact. For Hindus, the Himalayas are not just an awe-inspiring mountain range but also a highly-revered holy monument. I had grown up with millions of sacred pictures in my life and the one of Lord Shiva in front of the snow-covered Himalayas was firmly embedded in my memory.

Once we reached cruising altitude, our flight attendant passed out a leaflet with details of all the mountain peaks we would see on our flight. The sketches in the booklet matched precisely the scenery outside. As the peaks became clearer in the rays of the rising sun, I could see why this mighty mountain range had mesmerized poets and authors for centuries.

I kept my nose pressed against the window so as not to miss a thing. As the plane moved closer to the mountains, the view outside became more and more spectacular. After a few minutes, the sharp peak of Gauri-Shankar came into view. This was a spiritually significant site for Hindus, as Lord Shiva and his consort Gauri were said to protect the mountain.

"You'll see Mount Everest in a couple of minutes," the flight attendant said in her Nepalese accent.

As we approached the mountain, I did not see a towering peak standing alone. Mount Everest was not as imposing as I had imagined. Since the peaks surrounding it were also very tall, Everest looked just marginally higher. But the experience of seeing the highest point on earth was something I will never forget. Once I set my eyes on Everest, it seemed to dominate my view as it loomed in front and dwarfed everything else.

There was something magical about that first view of Mount Everest. The history, the stories, the legends; they all flashed in my mind.

"How far are we from Everest?" I asked the flight attendant.

"About five miles," she said. I was surprised, as I felt we were much further away.

As I kept my face pressed against the window, I felt a tap on my shoulder. It was the attendant.

"If you'd like, you can go inside the cockpit for a closer view," she said.

I jumped from my seat in ecstasy and rushed to the front of the plane. The windows of the cockpit offered an even more comprehensive view of the mountain range. The day was bright and sunny and we had a clear view, with peaks appearing like distant Gothic castles in the air. We were fortunate. All other Everest flights that day were canceled due to inclement weather and low visibility.

After the flight, as Mamatha and I walked together on the tarmac, I felt so grateful that her pilgrimage had led to this unforgettable adventure. "Thank you for this trip," I said, putting my arm around her. Mamatha smiled and squeezed my hand.

I do not think I will ever climb to the top of Mount Everest. So I felt elated and fulfilled that I was able to appreciate the mountain from above. It was a once-in-a-lifetime experience. The feeling of tranquility from drifting through the haunting Himalayas lasted the whole day. It had been like watching a movie about the architectural creativity of God.

CHAPTER 8

To Hilsa by Helicopter

By the time we returned to the hotel, it was around ten in the morning. We were scheduled to catch a flight for Nepalgunj that afternoon. Enormously content, I took a short nap, the images of the Himalayan range and of Everest still lingering in my mind.

The Nepali city of Nepalgunj borders with the state of Uttar Pradesh in India and resembles a typical small Indian town. The Nepalgunj airport lies four miles to the north of the city and has direct flights to and from Kathmandu. When we arrived, Nepalgunj was very hot and we were sweating by the time we exited the plane and walked across the tarmac to the airport.

Our Nepalese tour guide received us at the airport with his shirt unbuttoned and his paunch open to the sky. It was as if he were using his tummy as a cooling fin, like a reptile from ancient times. After some confusion, we were taken to a van which drove us to our hotel.

Hotel Siddhartha looked quite posh from outside. Our room was fairly clean but it was hotter than outside as the air conditioner only blew hot air. The front window looked out onto a muddy pond surrounded by garbage and there were a few stray dogs and buffalos combing for food. I opened the window and pulled down the shades, hoping that the breeze from outside would cool the room. But the air outside was as still as a Yogi's mind.

Our flight to Simikot was supposed to be in the morning. There was no definitive departure time but we had to be up and ready by 8:00 a.m. It was only five in the evening and I figured I had plenty of time for a good eight-hour slumber. I took my shower, drank two pints of 'Everest Premium' Beer, ate some chicken sides and hit the sack by 8:00 p.m.

Even at night, the room was so hot that Mamatha and I kept tossing throughout the night. We were ready to check out by 7:00 a.m. the next morning and I called the reception to send porters. No one answered. As it turned out, we had to carry our own bags as the porters had not yet reported for work. While I was busy emptying my last rectal remains of the previous day's dinner, Mamatha moved our luggage all the way to the reception, huffing and puffing to the lobby through the small elevator with all her acrobatic skills. Luckily for me, when I joined her at the reception she only commented, "You and your toilet time."

The forty-three people in our group stood together, stranded outside the Nepalgunj airport. Only those passengers with boarding passes were allowed inside. We did not have our air tickets, let alone boarding passes, and so we waited outside along with many other travel groups. This was normal for Nepal. Due to the low visibility and unpredictable weather conditions, air tickets were issued only after flight operations were confirmed.

There were no seats or benches outside the airport. Some travelers stood, some roamed around, and others sat on the ground. Mamatha and I were making ourselves comfortable on the curbstone of the driveway outside when Ganesh, one of the other members, came toward us excitedly. With a big smile on his face he said, "Mohan, sir, while searching for my duffle bag I heard something hilarious from a Delhi tourist."

"What?" I asked curiously.

"Last Tuesday, as a plane landed at this airport, a wild boar ran out and collided with the rear wheels of the aircraft. The boar died on the spot and the plane narrowly escaped a major accident."

"I don't believe it," I said, looking at him incredulously. Ganesh ran toward others to share the funny story.

"Mona, will the flights be safe?" Mamatha asked in a nervous voice.

"Don't worry, Mamatha. We'll be safe." I kept my fears to myself.

With at least three hours left to wait, I thought this would be an excellent opportunity to acquaint myself with other members of our group. I had noticed Ganesh hanging out with four men, and I was keen to know them all. I could see them chatting with each other and I walked toward them.

"How has it been so far?" I asked the closest man. He was in his forties, dark and fit-looking with an intelligent facc.

"Hello, sir," he said. "I am Akash Gowda. It has been okay so far."

I introduced myself and Gowda pointed to a tall, lean man with an untrimmed beard. "This is Sriram, he knows your nephew, Pavan."

"Hi. I am Mohan Ranga Rao," I said extending my hand.

Sriram greeted me, staring as if he were examining a rare specimen or a celebrity. "How is Pavan Ranga related to you?"

"I am his uncle" I said, smiling to myself. I was amused that my wealthy nephew was as well known in Mysore as a Rockefeller in New York.

Gowda continued, "This is Suri, he owns a rice mill in Sriranga Patna." He pointed to a tall man standing nearby. "Over there is Narayana, the manager at Nandi temple in Mysore."

After chatting for a while with Gowda, I went back and sat next to Mamatha. It was hot and sunny and minutes felt like hours. Three middle-aged men walked in front of us, glaring at a giant heap of duffle bags and looking for a porter. Mamatha and I had carried our own bags as we had been told there weren't any porter services available.

"You have to fetch your bags from the pile." I called out. "There are no porters."

The tallest man went to the heap of duffle bags and started pulling them out one by one while his friends stood behind looking lost.

"Here, let me help you," I said, standing up. "What are your bag numbers?" After a few minutes of searching, we retrieved three bags from the stack.

"Thank you. My name is Annadorai," the tall man said in a thick South Indian accent as I dumped their bags. "This is Mr. Shankaran and Mr. Prabhakar Reddy."

After an hour, Shashi and Neelakanta came out of the airport, accompanied by another man of medium height and lean frame.

"This is Shashi," Neelakanta announced.

A short man joined Shashi. Shashi addressed the group, "This is Sonu, our associate. He is here to help with the travel arrangements." The agent held a bundle in his hand which turned out to be boarding passes.

"The flights to Simikot are operated by three airlines," Neelakanta said. "The aircrafts can carry only eighteen passengers. So far, Sonu has been able to get thirty seats on two flights for our group. He has already collected the boarding tickets on our behalf."

"Can we have them now?" I asked.

"Not yet," he said. "There's no room inside the airport. Two flights will have to leave before we're allowed inside. I will give out the tickets once I show the passes to security."

After two flights had taken off, we were allowed inside the airport. As we entered, I was shocked to see that the small space was already jam-packed with more than a hundred people. Nepalgunj airport is small and the airport authorities do not see the need to provide any seating arrangements for travelers. The departure hall, arrival hall, departure gate, security line, and a shop were all packed inside the main building. People and their large duffle bags filled every inch of space. The airport shop carried plastic dolls and unbranded candies. The noise inside the airport rivaled a crowded wedding and made any conversation between Mamatha and me a monumental effort.

Inside the hall, Shashi and Neelakanta began distributing the boarding passes. They stood in two different corners and shouted out names amid the noise and mayhem. Just as I was about to point out their stupidity in both speaking at once, I faintly heard Shashi call our names and I ran over to collect our boarding passes. We had one of the coveted thirty spots on the plane and would not need to wait for a later flight.

Boarding passes safely in hand, Mamatha and I stood at one corner of the bustling hall and watched the international array of passengers: Europeans, Nepalese, Tibetan Monks, Indians and Sherpas. The Nepalese Sherpas were recognizable by the grocery items they carried, likely for trekkers' camps. For the Sherpas, security clearance was allowed for eggs and grains.

There was no restaurant or coffee shop at the airport, and Shashi distributed the *poori* and *bhaji* packets he had brought from the hotel. I opened the parcel to find pooris as thick as buns and potato slices with turmeric and toasted cumin seeds. I was starving and took half a poori and an *aloo bhaji* only to discover that it was rubbery and thick. I struggled to eat at least three bites, thinking it might grow on me, but I just could not chew the food into pieces small enough to swallow. I did not wish to appear snobbish, so I made a show of eating a couple of bites and then secretly packed the rest back in the plastic pouch and, when nobody was looking, I slipped the pouch into a nearby dustbin.

Due to the inclement weather, the forty-three members of our group could not all fly to Simikot on the same day. The last flights of the day were canceled and eight members were forced to stay back at Nepalgunj airport, not knowing when they would be able to fly out. A couple from Arsikere got separated, with the wife receiving a boarding ticket while the husband was left behind. They couldn't change places with another passenger in the group since, for security reasons, boarding tickets could not be exchanged.

"Mohan, I will go sit by that lady who is alone. She's from our group," Mamatha said as I returned from secretly disposing of the food.

"Sure," I replied, appreciating her sensitivity.

It can be daunting to travel alone, especially in crowded airports and stressful situations. Mamatha joined the woman and they exchanged pleasantries. Mamatha ended up accompanying the woman until the plane landed at Simikot and made her feel comfortable and secure throughout the journey.

Since there was no public address system or any display signs showing the status of flights, passengers had to constantly pay attention to the security staff at the two tiny departure gates. We had been waiting for a long time when suddenly Shashi appeared and signaled to everyone to get up and get ready to board the flight. No one seemed to know which exit to take. Mamatha, her new friend and I went to the nearest one and luckily it was the correct gate.

The clean interior of the relatively new Dornier aircraft from Tara Air felt safe, dispelling my apprehensions. The pilots who regularly fly at the low altitude of 10,000 feet are daring and skillful but nevertheless, there are frequent crashes between Nepalgunj and Simikot.

Although the distance was just slightly over 125 miles, the flight took about fifty-five minutes. The trip was scenic, with views of the river valleys and tropical forests of the Himalayan foothills. Looking out the window from several thousand feet above the mountains, for the first time during the trip I looked forward to the visual feast that awaited me the following week.

We landed at Simikot around 11:00 a.m. As the door opened, a cool breeze swept through the aircraft, replacing the hot Nepalgunj air.

Simikot is located in the northern tip of Nepal, bordering Tibet. It is twice the elevation of Kathmandu, and as soon as I exited the plane, I started feeling a slow, throbbing pain at the back of my neck. This is a common effect of high altitude and tour operators offer acetazolamide tablets to all pilgrims, which lessens the effects of altitude sickness.

I followed the other passengers down the ladder and looked around, searching for the airport. It was nowhere to be seen. There was only the tarmac and a small dilapidated building on a peak a short distance away. This building, as it turned out, was the airport.

As we climbed up the incline and approached the building, we came across two doors. One was the exit and the other led inside the airport. We passed through the departure gate, turned to our left and walked exactly three steps before reentering the airport.

A few hundred meters away from the tarmac I saw three helipads and about fifty people waiting. When our group arrived at the helipads, we were each weighed along with our luggage. There was an upper limit of eighty-five kilograms and if a passenger and their bags exceeded the limit they

needed to pay the fare for a second passenger. Mamatha and I both passed.

The Simikot departure zone was constructed of odd-sized boulders that also served as a barricade around the perimeter of the airport. Stone slabs and blocks of various sizes and shapes piled up and held together with wire mesh formed a low wall, perfect for sitting. I made myself comfortable on one of the slabs as Mamatha sighed and sat next to me.

I watched as about twenty-five passengers lined up to catch the next helicopter. Five or six passengers were boarded into each helicopter, depending on their size and weight. The round trip to Hilsa takes about twenty minutes and five helicopters were operating simultaneously to relay people there. The Tibetan branch of Shekar Treks had access to two helicopters, so only five or six of us could leave every half hour.

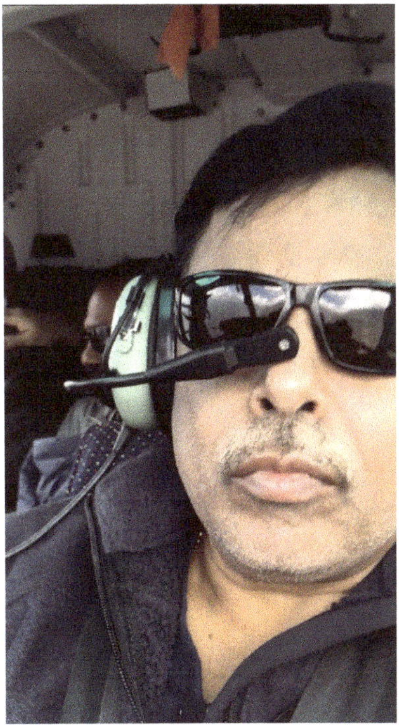

I

Although we were sitting exposed in the foothills of the Himalayas, it was sunny yet pleasantly cold. We had to wait for an hour and a half before our group's turn came. Then we formed a line for boarding. Six of us: Ganesh, Narayan, Akash, Sriram, Mamatha and I, got into the second 'copter. It was a red helicopter and seemed pretty solid. I was seated next to the pilot and got to wear the co-pilot's headphones. The exchanges overheard between the pilot and the control center in the local language added to the exciting experience. From my seat, I had an incredible view of the Himalayan ridges and the rivers flowing in the narrow valleys. I saw an entirely different landscape and a diverse Himalayan terrain. The ecosystem of the lower ranges varied, from pine trees on the heights and lush forests in the valleys. Some peaks appeared to pierce the sky and were surrounded by deep valleys and flowing rivers.

When we landed, I was the first to get out and I nearly fell as the swirling force of the wind from the helicopter's propellers knocked me off-balance. Mamatha, always more careful, wisely waited for the propellers to stop. When we were only about a hundred yards away, the helicopter took off again. The pilot made an expert U-turn between two mountain ranges in the narrow valley before disappearing from sight.

With the helicopter gone, there was a sudden stillness broken only by the gentle sound of the Karnali River and the blowing of the wind. We moved closer to the riverbank and I saw that the Karnali appeared to be flowing faster and with more turbulence than any river I had seen before. The fresh air hit my nostrils within seconds as the wind blew with bone-chilling gusts.

There was an altitude gain of 3,500 feet between Simikot and Hilsa. Taking into account the altitude gain from Nepalgunj to Simikot, in a matter of hours we had climbed from less than 500 feet in Nepalgunj to 12,000 feet at Hilsa. After taking the acetazolamide tablets this did not cause a problem for any of us and no one complained.

I inhaled deeply through my nose and exhaled through my mouth, to experience deep breathing at a high altitude. Mamatha followed suit. We only carried our backpacks; our duffle bags, left at the airport, would be delivered later by Sherpas.

The six of us started walking. We didn't know which direction we should be going and there wasn't a soul—human or animal—in sight. The terrain was dry, with brown gravel and sand all around us. There were no trees and the ground resembled a desert.

Miles of eternal nothingness stretched to my right, so I decided to take the trail that headed left. To the left, we could see the trail for a few hundred yards and then it wound out of sight. We walked around the curve and I was relieved to see a hamlet come into view. This was our first experience with high-altitude trekking on this trip. We were at 12,000 feet, but it felt no different than a regular stroll in the park in my hometown of Mysore.

"Pick a nice spot for tomorrow's crap," I joked, as we looked at the rocky surroundings.

"Somewhere behind one of these big rocks," said Akash.

"Make sure your bottom is way above the ground," I laughed. "And get used to covering it with sand. We have left the land of flushing."

CHAPTER 9

A la Indiana Jones

Hilsa is a tiny hamlet, situated in a beautiful valley between two mountain ranges with the Karnali River running in between. "That part is China-controlled Tibet," Sriram pointed out, gesturing to the mountain range on our left.

As we approached Hilsa, I was reminded of villages in the remote rural areas of my home state, Karnataka. The only difference was that in Karnataka, people lived in thatched huts and the buildings in Hilsa were gray and appeared more impoverished.

Hilsa is a seasonal town on the Nepal-Tibet border. There were fewer than twenty buildings including the customs and immigration office. Most people in Hilsa work in the hospitality business, as pilgrims and trekkers, mostly from India, use this route to go to Mount Kailash. During winter, the town is covered in thick snow. Hotels shut down and most of the population moves to a lower elevation. The residents return in March when the tourist season resumes and then stay until September or October.

As we entered the main village, we were immediately hit with the stench of human excretion. Obviously, with the cold nights and dark early mornings, most pilgrims just used spots around the village for discharging their waste.

"Tomorrow there will only be two places in Hilsa," I announced, "the place to sleep and the place to crap." Everyone burst out laughing.

The guesthouse, where we had to wait before proceeding to Takalkot, was called Kailash Hotel and Resorts. However, if one arrived with any preconceived notion of a resort or a hotel, one would be sorely disappointed. To the left of the entrance was a shop selling biscuits and water. Right behind the shop counter was a small kitchen, which contained a gas stove with two burners and a few large cooking utensils. A doorway in the back opened onto a dormitory with eight mattresses on cots, without sheets or pillows.

The entire structure was constructed out of mud, with unfinished floors covered with jute carpet. A large aluminum pot with boiling water and sliced potatoes was kept on a gas stove in the open courtyard. Right behind the pot was a running tap with a wet piece of cloth slung around its mouth to prevent splashing. Neelakanta, who was making this trip for the "umpteenth" time, told me that compared to the facilities for pilgrims available a few years ago, this "modern" hotel was practically luxurious.

A group of six members had already taken two of the six single beds in the nearest dormitory. Mamatha and I took one of the remaining beds, setting our bags on the bare mattress.

Dinakar and Rajasri, the siblings we had seen in Kathmandu, entered the room and each occupied a cot.

As we settled in, Dinakar introduced himself to the group. "I'm a software engineer working for Oracle in America, in Denver. My sister, Rajasri, is a hospital administrator and lives in Bangalore."

On another cot, two men were sitting next to each other. The taller man came over to me, extended his hand and said, "I am Arun. I know your brother Mr. Guru very well."

"I have six brothers," I replied, reaching out to shake his hand. "Guru is my eldest."

"I know him from Rotary."

I later found out that Arun was one of the founders of a large IT company and had taken a voluntary retirement after receiving several hundred million shares.

By the time we settled in, it was around noon. Neelakanta had told us the hotel would serve lunch at 2:00 p.m., which meant that we had two hours to wait.

We all lay on our bare cots. There was no television, radio or books. It was like a reality show with twelve adults stranded inside a large room with cold weather outside and only each other for amusement. We weren't sure how long we would be in the hotel, since we had to wait for everyone from our group to arrive before proceeding to our next destination.

A middle-aged couple entered our room along with a young man who appeared to be their son. They took a long look around the room and at the occupied cots. As they turned to leave, I moved closer to Mamatha on the bed we were sharing.

"Please stay," I said, "There's plenty of room."

Dinakar got up and sat next to his sister, leaving a whole cot for the family.

"I'm Shetty," the man introduced himself as he sat down on the empty bed. He pointed to his companions. "This is my wife and son."

"Where are you from?" I asked.

"We're from Karwar."

Another eight members joined us shortly and soon there were about twenty people in the two adjoining rooms.

"Do you know that this village has no water supply, no electricity, and no sewage system?" Dinakar mused.

"Then where is the tap water coming from?" Arun asked.

"There's a small stream about a hundred feet above here. Someone fitted a plastic Coke bottle with its bottom rim cut off and attached a hose to the mouth of the container."

"That makes sense," Arun said. "I saw the plastic tank on the roof."

Rajasri closed her eyes in contemplation and started to quietly chant a Sanskrit hymn. Everyone else was silent for a few minutes. Then I asked Dinakar, "Is this your first trek?"

"No, I'm a regular trekker. I've done over a hundred treks, mostly in Colorado."

A large family sitting on two cots was chatting noisily in Telugu and suddenly they all burst out laughing. Their joyful relationship reminded me of my own large family of twenty-two who lived together under one roof before I got married. I addressed the family, "If you speak in Kannada, we can also enjoy your joke. You are from the Shekar Treks group, right?"

"Yes, we all are," said the man who had narrated the joke, "I am Nagaraj." He shook my hand and introduced me to his parents, his three brothers, and their wives.

I asked the group, "Does anyone here know why the southern range of the Himalayas is called the Mahabharat Hills?"

Dinakar replied, "According to the Puranas, the ancient texts, five Pandava brothers are believed to have spent their thirteen years of exile in this region of the Himalayan foothills."

Arun asked, "Did not the Pandavas take this same route while making the final journey of their lives?"

"Yes," Rajasari responded. "According to Mahaprasthanika Parva, the last part of Mahabharata, the Pandavas, along with their shared wife Draupadi and the dog that befriended them trekked to the summit of Mount Kailash on their path to liberation, as it is considered to be a gateway to Heaven, also known as *Swarga Loka*."

"The four faces of Mount Kailash face the four directions of the compass," added Dinakar. "According to the Vedas, the mountain is a link between Heaven and earth. Even the followers of Buddhism and Jainism believe that the peak is a heavenly gate. Kailash is a library of mysteries and answers, like the Holy Grail in Christianity. The mountain emits strong positive energy in all the four directions and at sunset, the shadows cast by the mountain on the eastern side form a swastika, which in Hinduism represents well-being and prosperity.

"Reminds me of Indiana Jones and the last crusade where Indy encountered the Holy Grail," I said lightheartedly. Dinakar grinned. The others didn't get it.

We sat in silence for a moment, each thinking of the journey ahead. "I wonder what the true origins of the ancient Rishis were," Rajasri pondered without opening her eyes.

Dinakar responded, "No individual prophet was given credit for the Vedas, for they were perceived through revelatory vibrations during the periods of deep meditation of these sages."

Arun asked, "Is it true that significant benefits are derived from the vibrations that emanate from the correct chanting of Vedic hymns?"

"Mamatha and I carried out Rudra Homa at Ram Mandir in Mysore," I said.

"Did you experience any special sensations during the Rudra Homa?" Shetty asked.

"I was deeply moved and astounded by the vibrations of the collective chanting of twenty-one Brahmins."

Everyone seemed curious and eager to know more. "The sensations were surreal," I went on. "The whole ritual lifted my psyche to another zone. It was as if some sublime changes were happening deep inside my subconscious mind. Incidentally, that's what eventually resulted in us taking this trip to Kailash Manasa Sarovar."

CHAPTER 10

Altitudes and Yak Tea

"*Chai, chai*," a young Nepali man entered the room carrying small steel cups and a big aluminum kettle with a spout. He went around to each traveler, serving tea made from *nak*'s milk. A nak, or *dri,* is a female yak. The cup of nak's milk tea was very sweet and had more animal odor than the buffalo milk I used to drink with my Ovaltine when I was a kid. The tea was very thick and very hot. My dry mouth yearned for anything wet and warm, and without caring for politeness, I asked for another cup of the hot beverage before the kettle disappeared.

"*Sojavo mat, jaago! Jaago!* Don't sleep, wake up! Wake up!" the smiling youth yelled at the bearded man Nagraj while pouring his tea.

Nagraj, a hefty man in his forties, looked reasonably fit. He had been asleep on his cot and pretended to get up, but went back to bed as soon as the young man left the room. High altitudes will give you a headache if you lie down suddenly without correctly acclimatizing your body and the Nepali was following the age-old advice of the Sherpas, "Don't sleep suddenly at high altitudes; sleep only after a few hours of adjusting."

When we finished our tea, we rinsed the cups in the freezing tap water. I washed mine as quickly as I could but when I removed my hand from the running water it was already numb from the cold. Washing those cups was the first of many cold-water cleaning experiences—internal and external—in the days to come. Although the outside temperature was around ten degrees Celsius, the tap water came from melting mountain snow and glaciers. When they were rinsed, we placed the teacups back on the large wooden table laid out in the central courtyard.

It was now more than two hours since our arrival into Hilsa and we were still waiting for the last eight members of our group to fly down from Simikot. By 2:00 p.m., we were all familiar with each other and the group members no longer felt like strangers. Nagraj was still napping, not heeding the advice about acclimatizing first. Suddenly, he got up from the bed, staring blankly and unable to stand upright. He sat on the edge of the bed with his head bent down. "I have an unbearable pounding headache," he said.

"Do you feel giddy?" Dinakar asked.

Nagraj cocked his head and raised his eyebrows, trying to focus.

"Why don't you consult Ganesh?" I suggested. "He's a physiotherapist and is carrying a bagful of medicine, including injections for emergencies."

Nagaraj sat with his head still hanging down in an apparent attempt to prevent dizziness. He thanked me and slowly got up, stumbling to the next room. His brother-in-law ran behind him, holding his shoulders to steady him.

A critical danger of trekking at high altitudes, particularly in the Southern Himalayas, is the sudden change in ambient temperature. The deadly combination of high altitude and an unexpected drop in temperature plays havoc with untrained Kailash pilgrims and often takes their lives. Above 10,000 feet, the oxygen level in the atmosphere drops by about 10% for every 2,000-foot gain in elevation. As an example, although the oxygen content on Mount Everest is the same as in Mumbai, due to the low atmospheric pressure, on Everest only about 30% of the available oxygen can enter our lungs.

When the external pressure becomes too low, some individuals suffer adverse reactions. Their internal organs expand from the pressure difference between their bodies and outside, causing high-altitude cerebral edema (HACE), a unique and life-threatening condition. This results in hypoxia, a condition in which the body or a region of the body is deprived of adequate oxygen supply at the tissue level. A minor form of this is called "acute mountain sickness" (AMS). Often high-altitude trekkers will bring Erythropoietin (EPO) injections, which have an especially curative effect in counteracting hypoxia.

Nagaraj soon returned after getting his treatment. He looked less unsteady but lay down on the cot again, despite protests from his wife. Nagaraj was not the only traveler who felt ill; the sudden altitude gain of over 12,000 feet in a day had produced altitude sickness in quite a few of us.

Govind, the tour leader, had not yet joined us. There was nobody to guide the group or to assist members in distress. We were not sure if Neelakanta and Shashi were volunteers or paid staff and if they were responsible for the welfare of the members.

Ganesh, the physiotherapist, had been complaining of severe headaches. I recalled how a young trekker had died in his sleep after returning from Kardungla pass at an altitude of 12,000 feet in Ladakh. Sleeping right after a sudden ascent into high altitude can cause blood pressure to plunge and can bring on dangerous reactions in some people. Fortunately, none of our group had gotten into serious trouble so far.

Experts on acute altitude sickness have a mantra: "If you have a headache, don't ignore it." They also warn travelers visiting high altitudes to be on the lookout for loss of balance, a sign their condition may be worsening. This, along with a lingering headache, could be the beginning of an edema, a swelling in the brain.

Doctor Jan Stepanek, chair of the American Aerospace Medical Program, advises: "The best treatment for any altitude-caused condition is to descend, descend, and descend. Going down 500 meters, about 1,500 feet, doesn't sound like much—but that increase in pressure and improvement in oxygen delivery can make a world of difference." The problem in Hilsa was that the only way to descend was by helicopter.

It was around 2:30 p.m. We were scheduled to take a quick lunch and then proceed to Takalkot in Tibet by crossing the border on a long suspension bridge connecting Tibet and Nepal. Two buses would be waiting to pick us up about a mile into Tibet. But there was a hitch. Since we carried a visa with the names of all the group members on one permit, we all needed to enter China together. Unfortunately, eight from our group were still stranded at Nepalgunj due to the lack of flights to Simikot. Would the eight missing comrades join us in time to leave for Takalkot by that evening? No one knew.

I went to talk to Neelakanta, since he was the one who had distributed the boarding passes.

"What now, Neelakanta?" I asked.

"Why are you asking me?" he said, looking angry. "I'm just another traveler."

His response left us wondering if Neelakanta was a group member like the rest of us who had paid the full trip expenses or if he was a hired hand from Shekar Treks. There was no person to direct the next course of action and we looked at each other for answers.

Suddenly I felt an urge to pee and I hurried outside, stopping about a hundred steps from the hotel. The experience of emptying my bladder in the middle of the Himalayas with the view of the legendary Karnali flowing nearby added a spiritual dimension to a mundane routine. As I looked at the surrounding landscape I felt a sense of exhilaration, like a unique creature marking its territory.

When I returned, Dinakar was saying, "Isn't it incredible how the sources of four of the largest rivers of India—Ghagra, the main tributary of the Ganges, Sutlej, Indus, and Brahmaputra—are within the vicinity of Kailash?"

Dinakar began describing some of the stories about Lord Shiva and Mount Kailash when a sudden howling wind outside caught the attention of everyone in the room and an eerie silence enveloped the group.

Many myths swirled around Kailash, elevating the reverence people felt for the mountain. To me, such devotion to a mountain appeared delusional. I did not wish to fall into this trap of building up the place in my mind. "I would rather find out for myself than blindly believe in legends and myths," I said.

"Why, you don't believe our epics?" Shetty asked.

"I do," I said cautiously and paused before elaborating. "But believing in our epics based merely on their legends would be blind faith. For me to believe in something, I need to experience it myself."

"You do not believe in God?"

"Yes," I replied. "But I came on this trip more for the physical endeavor and scenery of the trek than for religious reasons."

I had to keep reminding myself not to be casual about the trek or to make comments that might hurt the feelings of the other members. To me, the Kailash trek was a physical challenge, a sightseeing destination located at high altitude rather than a great pilgrimage worthy of reverence.

"And you, Mamatha?" asked Dinakar.

"A close friend of mine told me to undertake the Parikrama after Mohan and I carried out Rudra Homa," she said, in her slow and meticulous style, not divulging that it was a death threat that triggered this adventure. "My friend said that very few people were lucky enough to carry out a Rudra Homa along with twenty-one Brahmins and a Vedic pundit and that a Parikrama around Mount Kailash would be a great conclusion."

"What about you, Dinakar?" I asked "Why did you undertake this trip?"

"My sister and I were both fascinated by Mount Kailash and we had promised each other that we would go together one day, so here we are."

"And you, Arun?" I turned to the millionaire businessman.

"My daughter has a problem with one of her eyes, a condition called "lazy eyes." My father-in-law consulted a Vedic pundit and he advised me to undertake this trip for her welfare."

"I'm sure Lord Shiva will bless her with all the health in the world," said Mr. Shetty, bringing his hands together. "The Kailash Manasa Sarovar has been on our bucket list for many years. My wife has been dreaming about it and we wanted to complete it before we got too old."

"I am mainly here for the holy dip in Manasa Sarovar. It has been my dream," said Prakash, a food distributor.

For me, the trip had started to feel like an austere vacation with a bunch of extremely pious individuals. I did not share the passion or the religious reverence of my fellow group members but was constrained to pretend that I did. I pushed myself back on the cot to sit straight against the wall. I then closed my eyes, planning to carry out my breathing drills.

Hysterical shouts outside broke the silence and I reluctantly opened my eyes. We all ran outside to find out what was going on. The guesthouse was situated in a valley between two mountain ridges. Close to the guesthouse was a small, barren mountain peak about a thousand feet tall. The peak rose almost vertical with a steep incline and the terrain was slippery and treacherous.

Neelakanta was staring at the summit and shouting angrily. We looked up and saw a man in a red jacket halfway up the ridge, climbing to the summit of the mountain. Hearing Neelakanta's frantic shouts, he stopped and turned around, gripping a large boulder.

"Get down, I say!" Neelakanta screamed. "You're going to die, you idiot!"

Dinakar said, "He looks like the guy from Hyderabad."

"Yes. That is Prasanna from Hyderabad," affirmed someone else. "Doesn't he know it's very dangerous to climb peaks not frequented by the locals? Besides, we're supposed to acclimatize today and tomorrow with complete rest."

"Come back here at once, you ass!" Neelakanta screamed again.

I understood why Neelakanta was so furious. People frequently die from ignorance about altitudes and landslides. The authorities would hold the travel agent responsible if something happened to Prasanna.

Prasanna turned around again and saw us waving and frantically beckoning him to get back. He slowly started descending and we waited for him to reach us. When he was safely off the peak, Prasanna approached us with a surprised look and an expression that said, "What did I do wrong?"

Neelakanta leaned in, close enough to bite off Prasanna's nose. He stopped just short of slapping Prasanna in the face. "What the hell do you think you're doing?" he shouted, furious. "Who permitted you to leave the guesthouse? If you die through your stupidity, I'll be put behind bars. That's it, you're going back to Bangalore. Pack up and leave."

Prasanna reached out and took Neelakanta's hands, pleading for forgiveness. "Sorry, sir. Sorry, sir! I asked people sitting here and they said it was okay for me to go up."

Neelakanta turned away. "No, you're going back immediately. That's it."

"Sir, please. Sir, I will not go anywhere. I promise. I promise," Prasanna begged.

Neelakanta was in no mood to relent. "You're going back, and that's it," he snapped before storming off.

Of course, there was no way to send Prasanna back unless Neelakanta found a yak and driver.

"It's like the Telugu movie *Bahubali,"* I said to the others. "Where Bahubali tries to climb a massive mountain to meet the lover of his dreams."

For the rest of the trip Prasanna was nicknamed, "Bahubali."

When I returned to the room, a mild-mannered man in his forties introduced himself to me. "I am Suresh," he said. "I'm from Chikkaballapur. I was the distributor of your Vasu range of convenience foods. People are still missing your food products. Why did you sell off that business, sir?"

Suresh was the millionth man to ask me that very same question and I did not have the patience for a long and complicated explanation. I had sold the company after I lost my eldest daughter to cancer and was in a deep financial crisis. Thinking of this reminded me that my main grudge against worship was because the only day I religiously carried out *Ganesha puja* at home turned out to be the most tragic day of my life. Right after the puja, I received the diagnosis of my eight-year-old daughter's leukemia. I did not want to revisit those terrible days of my past.

Without answering, I got up from the cot and stood looking out the window, seeking a diversion. Just then, Ganesh entered the room. He announced, "The latest information is that eight from our group are still waiting at Nepalgunj airport."

"My God," Mamatha said, "They will still need to take the helicopter to Hilsa. Will they be able to make it today?"

"Let us hope so," said Arun.

"Looks like we may have to stay here tonight," I said.

"We *will* have to stay here tonight," Arun corrected me.

I looked around. There was not even enough room for people to sit comfortably, let alone sleep. Just as we were discussing the prospect of finding enough space, we heard helicopters arrive. We were hopeful it would be our missing eight, but instead, to our horror, a group of eleven people from another tour group entered the guesthouse. There were already more than fifty people in the eight-room guesthouse, and these additional trekkers further complicated matters.

"Let me go and hold a room with enough mattresses for us upstairs," I said. A bond had formed between the people in the room. We all had a common purpose, common apprehensions, common high-altitude problems, and, most importantly, common toilet concerns. And together, we had all slowly started to forget the mundane and to anticipate an experience like nothing we'd ever had before.

I was about to leave the room when Neelakanta entered. "Please cover your head," He said, looking at my bare head.

"We will not serve lunch to those who do not cover their heads. The weather here is very treacherous. If your head is not kept warm, you will easily fall ill."

Neelakanta was not wearing a hat, and to lighten up the mood I sang the popular song, "*Heluvudu Ondu Maaduvudu Innondu*", which contained the lyrics, "preaching one thing and doing exactly the opposite." Everyone laughed, including Neelakanta.

"When is lunch?" I asked Neelakanta, looking at my watch. It was past two and I was hungry and ready to eat.

Neelakanta smiled and said that lunch was ready to be served at any time. He added, "By the way, Mr. Gopinath became dizzy and collapsed. But he's okay now and is resting." Gopinath was the husband of the couple from Bangalore who had arrived at Hilsa before us.

"That's the problem with bringing older people on a trip like this," Rajasri said.

"What is your dividing line for old people?" Mamatha asked.

Rajasri thought for a while and replied, "Anyone close to sixty."

Mamatha smiled. "Well, for your information, Mohan is fifty-eight."

Rajasri covered her mouth with her right palm. "I'm sorry," she said in an apologetic tone. "You don't look that old at all."

"One of the eight stranded at Nepalgunj airport is cursed," Neelakanta said, changing the subject. "Because of this, we're all suffering. We would be sleeping on cozy beds at Takalkot if not for that individual."

Trying not to laugh, I shook my head at Neelakanta. Then Mamatha and I went down to lunch.

We had two options for lunch: dhal and rice, or dhal and pulka. I wondered what had happened to the boiling potatoes I had seen when we arrived at the guesthouse. But thanks to my ravenous hunger, lunch tasted like food from the heavenly kitchen of Kailash.

The rice was steaming and slightly pasty and the dhal was spiced just right with no fat. Even though they were serving hot water, I drank directly from the cold tap. Many others refused to touch the tap water, including Ganesh who drank only bottled mineral water.

After lunch I noticed that Ganesh was missing. I went looking for him, as I was keen to join their gang for a round of rummy. I found him in his room, lying on one of the beds. "My splitting headache is not going away, even after several painkillers," he groaned.

I replied, "Get up, doc. Don't you know you're not supposed to lie down until your body gets adjusted to the altitude?"

Ganesh ignored me, as he did not like receiving health advice from a non-medical person. I went back to my room and sat next to Mamatha.

"Mohan," Mamatha said softly in my ear, "it looks like we'll have to spend the night here. Why don't you check out the sleeping facilities?"

I went out to assess our options. There were six rooms on the ground floor and I started with the room right next to us. The room contained fourteen single cots with cotton mattresses and a pillow on each. Bundled up on the ground in a corner were a few cushions.

I wondered how others were managing and I went to the adjacent room to check on the Mysore gang. I could only peek inside with my hands on the doorframe as there was no space for me to enter with four cots wedged next to each other. The mattresses looked like they were last washed when Buddha was alive. Ganesh was sleeping and I shook him and reminded him to get up so his head would be vertical.

"A severe headache," he murmured without moving, his back to me.

The other men were playing rummy. "Good luck," I said, waving at them from the doorway.

"We may have to sleep outside," I announced when I was back in my room.

"Sleeping outside is no joke," Arun said. "The climate here is extremely unpredictable, changing every few minutes. It may drop to sub-zero temperatures at night for all we know and we may end up with acute pneumonia tomorrow."

The "resort" was so packed that there was only one thing we could do: sleep bum-to-bum, swallowing our vanity and shyness. Rich or poor, old or young, fit or unfit, all of us had to learn to survive and manage the available resources. We were learning to surrender to an unknown force and this night was a test of our commitment and grit.

I continued my search for bedding. Climbing the stairs to the second floor, I found a toilet where the staircase ended. I looked inside and recoiled in horror. The only area in the whole bathroom that was not filthy was the empty bucket below the tap. Every other place was covered with some form of human output. One good thing about extreme cold weather was that it made the nasty smell almost bearable.

At first it appeared that all the guestrooms were fully occupied, but in one room on the second floor I discovered a few people sitting on a veritable carpet of mattresses laid out wall-to-wall without any gap between them. There were a few vacant mattresses and those gave me a ray of hope. We were about thirty-five in our group and only about fifteen of us had found a nest.

I went back down to our room and brought Mamatha upstairs to the room carpeted with mattresses. There were also a few pillows and thick blankets. Dinakar and his sister followed us, as did the family of three from Karwar. That left twelve from our group remaining without beds.

Dinner was at 8:00 p.m. sharp and as we ate Mamatha and I stood shivering, our hands warmed by the plates piled with piping hot rice and dhal. At 8:30 p.m. we all went to bed. The mattresses were so small that Mamatha and I almost had to cling together and the air in the small room rang with snores and farts.

That day was a great reminder to me of how little a person actually needs: a basic lunch and supper, no toilet or hot water, a crowded mattress on the floor without a heater or adequate pillows. It is said that people do not freely choose to travel to Mount Kailash. That Kailash chooses you, not the other way round. On a journey to a great destination, the body and soul should not be concerned with the considerable challenges of the trip. What the mind accepts, the body understands. And undertaking the journey to Kailash Manasa Sarovar Yatra is a way to wholeheartedly comprehend the depth of this philosophy.

"Why spend a minor fortune to undergo this hardship?" I thought for a moment. Then I shook my head and decided to stay positive. "This trip will be a new experience, unlike any of the trips in my life. No wonder it is called 'Kailash Yatra.' Yatra means journey and this is supposed to be a journey of self-discovery for both the mind and the body."

I slept like an angel.

CHAPTER 11

A Crappy Adventure

I awoke to snoring so loud that it sounded like the sawing of hard wood. I was dressed in thermals, my cotton shirt, and my brown woodland jacket. Still, it felt cold when I moved and the air in the crowded room was putrid and stale. I reached inside my inner jacket pocket and took out my smartphone, checking the time. It was five in the morning.

"Mamatha," I whispered softly. Mamatha was sound asleep.

Slowly and quietly, I got out of bed. I groped behind my pillow until I found my backpack. Using the flashlight from my pack, I took off my gloves and pulled out my headlight. Then I quietly stood up and headed for the door.

The corridor outside was narrow and open to the sky on one side. I put on my balaclava and strapped the headlight around my forehead. It was freezing and pitch dark. No one was awake, not even the hotel staff. I decided to explore the toilet before venturing outside since there was a remote chance the caretakers might have cleaned it during the night. But the toilet appeared dirtier than before and had clearly been used since I last checked.

So, I had to relieve myself in the dark expanse of the freezing Himalayas. At first, I hesitated, but then became delighted when I realized I would be contributing to the Himalayan undergrowth through my manure. I left the building and stood shivering outside for a few minutes, allowing my body to become accustomed to the cold. Then I got a sudden and rushing urge in my posterior for my morning call. With that, I commenced the first of the numerous Himalayan 'project craps.'

Though the full moon was just two days away, the clouds obscured the moon and darkened my surroundings. The ground was uneven and full of gravel and boulders. The LED headlight beam was powerful but still I walked carefully, following a trail that wound uphill. The steep inclination of my path meant that I was climbing up a peak. I split my attention between focusing the flashlight on my trail to watching my step, aware that I was climbing through an obstacle-laden terrain. I found it very difficult to coordinate focusing the headlight, following the narrow trail in the dark, keeping a firm grip on my toilet kit, and making sure I did not bump into a rock or step on something foul.

I walked until I was about six hundred feet from the guesthouse, as I didn't think anyone else would have ventured that far. Then I selected a spot behind a big rock. It was about forty feet higher than my starting point and the landscape up ahead looked vaguely like the silhouette of a peak in the darkness. I focused my flashlight on the boulder and sat behind it, placing the box of wet wipes next to me on the ground. I pulled down my three layers of clothing and a great gush of cold air blasted my lower parts, stiffening them.

I squatted down, country-style, and soon felt the comforting warmth of my urine passing between my thighs.

After ensuring that my colon was empty, I pulled out several wet wipes. To my utter surprise and pleasure, the wet wipes gave me a greater sense of cleanliness and softness than water. And due to the creamy moisturizer used in the wipes, there was no dryness around my butthole. I got up, and, steadying myself, pulled up my undergarment, thermals, and cargo trousers, buttoning and buckling myself up. Then I looked back at my performance. I was satisfied. I would not have to worry about my load for the next twenty-four hours.

There are many advantages to defecating in the open. First off, there are plenty of spots to choose, including: riverside, foothill, uphill, and between two boulders. It is fantastic to be under the open sky, especially in its near-ethereal state at dawn when the stars peep through the clouds. You can see how well you have done. You get to stretch your muscles because of your squat. And finally, you save so much water which otherwise would have gone down the drain, flushing away your biodegradable excrement.

When I was once again fully dressed, I headed back to the "resort" to wash my face and brush my teeth. It was still dark and freezing. As I reached the guesthouse, I saw candlelight inside the shop and a Nepalese man emerged from the store. I approached him and asked him where to brush my teeth by showing him my toothbrush and paste. He pointed to a small empty bucket that had been placed on a plastic stool.

"Collect the water from the tap," he said in broken Hindi.

I took the pail and filled it with water. Cleaning my face without a mirror and brushing my teeth in the dark using cold water was another new experience. As soon as I removed my gloves, my fingers started to feel numb. I rubbed them vigorously, blowing on them to keep them warm. The bristles on my toothbrush had frozen and become very hard and brushing simply caused the paste to smear on my teeth. The plastic bucket of water was too large to use as a mug, so I filled my cupped hand with cold water to rinse my mouth. My fingers were numb by the time I finished. I wanted a bath, but that was out of the question.

I returned to my bed lighter and cleaner but shivering from the cold. Mamatha was awake, lying curled up on the mattress. Under her balaclava, only the tip of her long red nose was visible.

"Finished?" she asked, her mouth covered with the thick woolen blanket.

"Yup. Quite an experience," I said, pulling the blanket over my head.

When the daylight started streaming into the room, Mamatha got up and went down with her brush and paste. After tossing and turning for a few minutes I got out of bed and followed her downstairs.

It was 6:30 a.m. and the place was buzzing with people carrying their kits and their towels. Watching the number of people in line for the dirty toilet, I felt happy that I had already finished my morning chores.

At 7:00 a.m., the Sherpa came with the usual kettle of hot tea. This time yak tea tasted far better to me and I helped myself to three cups. Dinakar squatted in the hallway outside our room and chanted Rudra Mantra and the old couple from Karwar recited a Vedic hymn inside the room.

"I don't want to miss the divine lights that appear over Lake Manasa Sarovar," Rajasri said. "I wonder if it's true that the lights are angels roaming around."

I looked down, trying to hide my grin.

"Mr. Mohan, what is your definition of God?" Shetty asked, noticing my reaction.

I thought for a while before replying. "To me, God is an infinitely intelligent field that pervades everything everywhere."

"I think the Universe is trying to understand itself through us," Arun said. "That's why there's an innate quest for progress and knowledge among humans."

"This Kailash trek is my ultimate goal of life," Mrs. Shetty added, bringing the conversation back to the upcoming trek. "If I can complete the holy dip in Lake Manasa Sarovar and circle around Mount Kailash, my life will be complete."

I was astonished that a mere journey to a holy place could play such an incredibly important role in someone's life.

"They say we will be physically closest to Mount Kailash during the first day of the Parikrama," Mrs. Shetty continued. "I think I will return after that, after my holy dip in Manasa Sarovar is complete."

"Many guides fool the pilgrims into believing that since they have come up to Dirapuk and seen Kailash from its closest point, the rest of the Parikrama is immaterial," said Dinakar. "They get their full fee anyway."

Dinakar turned to Mrs. Shetty. "Make sure you carry some pure *ghee*, pure camphor and coconut oil. This is the driest, harshest and thinnest air you shall ever experience in your life. Dry nasal tracts often bleed and are best treated with pure ghee. Wear sunscreen and treat burnt skin with coconut oil. Karpoor or camphor wrapped in fine cotton will help you with breathing, since the ascent is rapid and steep for us living in the plains."

Mamatha asked, "Is it true that in the hour before the break of dawn, Lord Brahma is active? People living in tents have heard water splashing in Manasa Sarovar. They say these are angels in the guise of swans. Some have even heard the sounds of bangles and footsteps."

"There are stories that the *Sapta Rishis*, the seven sages mentioned in Indian mythology, come and bathe every morning at the Manasa Sarovar Lake," said Arun.

One belief that was common among all the group members was that the Kailash Parikrama was considered the ultimate religious accomplishment and was a sure way of attaining salvation.

"I wonder why praying and going around any holy site or shrine in a clockwise direction is considered holy," Mamatha wondered aloud. "One Parikrama is said to erase the accumulated sins of a lifetime."

"In fact, Tibetans go around Kailash in an anticlockwise direction," said Arun.

"Our holy Puranas state that there is no sin in the world that cannot be destroyed by circumambulation of shrines," replied Mr. Shetty.

I began to wonder if it was my own lack of faith that was unfounded and contrived. My view of this trip as a high-altitude trekking adventure began to change and I felt a newfound urge to see and experience the divine spiritual destination, the holy Mount Kailash, up close.

Even though I had begun to understand and connect with their reverence and faith, I still felt the urge to tell my fellow travelers to actually experience the sensations at these legendary places instead of blindly believing myths and interpretations. I have an unpleasant tendency to blurt out my incredulous statements whenever I am around people with blind faith. But this time I focused all my mental energy on keeping quiet. I did not want to dispel or lessen anyone's belief on this holy pilgrimage.

The sound of helicopters arriving was a joyful interruption to our conversation and we hurried outside. There we saw Prasad and Geetha from Bangalore and the elderly trio from Tamil Nadu.

"Where are the others?" I asked Prasad.

"They're arriving in the next helicopter."

Although we had been waiting almost a full day, the extra night spent at Hilsa had helped us get acclimatized to the 13,000-foot altitude.

By 9:30 a.m. all the group members had arrived and we set out to cross the border and enter Tibet. The immigration and customs office at Hilsa was another loosely-constructed stone structure, with only a small fluttering flag indicating it was an administrative building. Since we were leaving Nepal, we passed by the office and assembled by the customs check post. The check post was nothing more than a wooden pole with two men on either side of the bridge entrance. Sherpas had piled up our duffle bags at the gate for inspection. Once we were lined up, the customs men assigned us numbers in ascending order from the first person in line. These became our identification numbers and we wrote them in our passports.

As Mamatha and I stood waiting for our turn, we watched River Karnali sweep through the gap between Tibet and Nepal. What appeared beautiful and stunning to us visitors was sinister and dangerous for locals, who lived with the river and its annual threats of floods and landslides. A few steps away, a Nepalese man was sitting on a boulder near the bridge, smoking.

"I have not seen any river flow as furiously as Karnali," I said to him.

"Yes. It is both a boon and a bane for us," the Nepali replied in fluent Hindi.

"Why is that?"

"It's like hide and seek. It gives us life, but it destroys our homes too when it floods. For years we have lived alongside the river. Mostly with joy, but also with tears in our eyes."

Before I could respond, Neelakanta and Shashi waved their arms to get our attention. Shashi called out, "Please approach the bridge and form a line. Write your serial number and group list on your passports."

We lined up again in the order of our passport serial numbers for a customs check. After about twenty minutes, it was our turn. Mamatha picked up her bag and opened it for inspection. The officer, who wasn't wearing a uniform, gave the bag a cursory glance, shook it and squeezed the outside.

Mamatha waited as I finished my inspection and we followed the other travelers across the bridge. Most of the members hired frail-looking Sherpa women to carry their duffle bags. I was awed at how these female Sherpas carried two or more duffle bags with ease, even though each bag weighed over fifteen kilograms. Mamatha and I took our own bags over the bridge. Mamatha carried hers even though it was heavier and a bit of a struggle.

Mamatha never let me carry her bags, and the thought occurred to me that she would make an excellent Sherpa.

CHAPTER 12

Divine Intervention in the Form of Alcohol

The suspension bridge to enter Tibet, "the roof of the world," was only about 200 feet in length but it spanned a deep valley that separated Nepal and Tibet. The narrow bridge swayed as we stepped onto it, swinging from side to side as we walked across. It certainly felt as if we were at the top of the earth,

The bridge was entirely supported by anchors at either end and had no towers or piers. Additional light ropes placed at a higher level served as handrails. The Sherpa women not only carried duffle bags on their backs but also walked without using the fence to balance themselves. Mamatha held onto the rope railing on the side but I forced myself to carry my duffle bag and walk without the railing's support.

Far below, River Karnali appeared calm due to the widening of the banks between the two ridges. I had a spectacular view of the mountain ranges on both sides. As I stepped off the bridge and joined the group, I felt a strange tension in the air. The Chinese border patrol wearing immaculate uniforms and the towering watchtower made me feel like we had arrived at a cantonment, a military station. The road was wide and made of asphalt and a brand-new multi-story building was a dramatic contrast to the rough huts on the other side of the bridge.

Two buses were waiting for us about a mile from the suspension bridge. Once again, we lined up with our passports in hand. Another group was in front of us and I watched as their group was verified by the authorities.

We had been warned not to take photographs once we crossed the border, as the Chinese army had bases nearby and would confiscate cameras. A man from the other group foolishly started taking snaps of the surrounding area with his phone and I heard heavy footfalls as two armed Chinese soldiers came into view. They ran at the man from behind, confronted him angrily and took his camera away. Then they led him inside the building, holding him between them. After a few minutes, the man returned and announced that the guards had deleted all the pictures on his phone and had let him off with a warning.

When it was our turn, two Chinese immigration officers checked our documents, comparing each person's face against the photo on their passport. The procedure took about an hour.

After the officials were done, Neelakanta asked us for our passports. "The immigration officers will keep them for a few hours," he said. "But you will get them back by the end of the day. By the way, please do not wander off or take photographs. It's currently illegal to bring into China pictures, books, videos or speeches about or by the Dalai Lama. Images of the Tibetan national flag are even more illegal."

"Mohan, how can they take away our passports like that?" Mamatha asked. "What if they lose them?" If there was one thing that made Mamatha anxious, it was parting with her passport.

"There's no need to worry, Mamatha. Our passports will be safe," I said, trying to sound confident.

The driver of our bus was a handsome young man in a dark suit who looked like Jackie Chan. He didn't know a word of English. As soon as he started the van, he put on loud Chinese music, perhaps not realizing that the passengers were on a pilgrimage and that they preferred silence over Mandarin hip hop.

During the hour-long drive, none of us spoke. We just gazed outside at the barren yet beautiful landscape, with the snow-capped mountain range in the background. I thought about Tibet and China. In 1950, the newly established Chinese Communist regime decided that Tibet must become a permanent part of the People's Republic of China and launched an invasion. Tibetan resistance against the Chinese suppression started in 1959. The uprising was brutally quelled and the Dalai Lama was forced to flee into exile.

We soon arrived in the city of TakaTlkot. Chinese affluence had transformed the ancient Tibetan city into a clean and modern town with elegant buildings and excellent roads. The city resembled a small European township and our first stop was at the customs office, a plush, newly-constructed building.

We all got off the bus. It was bright and sunny with a strange mix of heat from the sun's rays and chilly weather from the low temperature. Neelakanta and Shashi assisted the driver in unloading the bags from under the bus. Each member then had to accompany their bag inside while it was scanned and inspected thoroughly. It took about an hour for my turn to come up and it was noon before we could proceed to our hotel.

My expectations of Tibet were all based on the Hollywood movie, *Seven Years in Tibet*. In the film, the whole of Tibet looked like an old country with only small houses and monasteries everywhere. Taklakot was utterly different, with paved roads and new shops on either side of the main street.

Our minibus stopped in front of a multi-storied building that looked more like a government office than a hotel. We all got off the bus and waited in the lobby.

A tall, dark man wearing glasses and a blue formal jacket with a turtleneck sweater approached us, holding a bundle of keys.

"Who is that?" I asked Arun.

"He is Govind, the owner of Shekar Treks and our main tour leader," Arun clarified.

"Those of you who find climbing stairs difficult at this high altitude please take rooms on the ground floor," Govind announced, after introducing himself.

Mamatha and I volunteered to take a room on the top floor. Our room, 407, looked clean and fresh and was a welcome respite after the night in Hilsa. We were scheduled to visit Lake Manasa Sarovar for the holy dip and the circumambulation of the lake the next morning. A good thing about the itinerary was that at each destination with an altitude gain of more than 2,000 feet, ample time was allowed for acclimatization. I felt a dull headache and as soon as I saw the bed, I removed my sneakers and collapsed on the crisp sheets. Mamatha joined me and we slept for an hour.

After forty-eight bathless hours, the hot shower at Taklakot felt heavenly and washed away all the dirt and dust of our long journey. I decided not to shave, to test out the myth about rapidly-growing hair in the vicinity of Mount Kailash. The shower made me sleepy, and as my headache was gone, I took another nap even though I knew it wasn't the best thing to do in this high altitude. Soon after, Mamatha shook me awake. "Get up. Sleeping will do you no good."

"Mamatha, what's happening?"

"The other members are inquiring about ATMs. Why don't you go out and get some money, Mona?" We had run out of Indian currency and the 1,000 euros we carried was of no use in Tibet. I grunted and turned in the bed, pulling the blanket close to my face. The thought of going out in the cold did not appeal to me. My eyes felt heavy and I was in no mood to get up.

"You're always like this," Mamatha raised her voice and shook me again. I got up with a grimace and put on my shoes.

I was tired and my head still ached, so climbing down fifty-four steps and walking 100 yards to the hotel gate required the mental effort needed to complete a marathon. By the time I reached the entrance, I was fed up with the ATM search. Nevertheless, I asked the security guard at the gate, "ATM?" Instead of responding, he turned away without even acknowledging my presence.

Next, I went to the shop beside the hotel, where there was a beautiful Tibetan girl behind the counter. "ATM?" I asked her.

"Huh?" she murmured, clearly wondering which item was called by that name in her shop.

I crossed the street looking for an ATM sign and took one long look down the road in both directions. There was not a single sign in English on any of the shops or buildings.

I returned to my room, swearing aloud to Mamatha, "What a shitty place. No one speaks English. I saw no ATMs anywhere." I took off my sneakers and collapsed on the bed, pulling the blanket over me.

Mamatha left and returned a few minutes later with 2,000 yuan. "Where did you even look?" she asked, slipping the currency in her purse while I pretended to be asleep. "There's a big bank just a hundred meters down the road."

Lunch was supposed to be at noon. Mamatha and I went to the dining hall near the lobby promptly at midday, only to be told that lunch was being served at noon Indian time, which was 2:30 p.m. in Taklakot.

"Mona, I don't feel like going back to the room. Why don't we go for a walk?" Mamatha asked.

"Sure," I said. "It will help us get used to the altitude."

As I mentioned earlier, the Universe has a way of making wishes come true if your intention is soulful. At the shop right next to the hotel, I found an entire rack of different varieties of Chinese liquor. The bottles were beautifully displayed, like statues of angels. The only English sign in town declared that

Chinese vodka was 45% alcohol. I bought half a liter. I didn't care how it tasted and I was excited as hell.

"I'm sure you're the only person to buy local alcohol on a pilgrimage," Mamatha mocked. We also bought some biscuits and canned orange juice and relished both.

"Why don't you open up your Endomondo app to keep track of your steps?" I cleverly changed the topic. Mamatha pressed the start button on her app and I tucked the bag with the vodka safely away. After we had walked for about twenty minutes it got very cloudy and at an altitude of nearly 13,000 feet, walking was noticeably more tiring than at the 3,000-foot altitude of Mysore, our hometown.

We went all around Taklakot and it was about two in the afternoon by the time we returned to the hotel.

"We've walked for about two miles," said Mamatha, checking her app.

Thanks to the biscuits and orange juice I had not found the stroll difficult. I felt secretly grateful to Mamatha for waking me up and dragging me out.

As we approached the gate of our hotel, we could hear loud noises emerging from reception. "We've been waiting here without rooms for more than an hour!" A bald gentleman from another group screamed at their tour leader.

"We urgently need to use the restroom," added a young woman.

It turned out that another group from Gujarat was experiencing a shortage of rooms. They were tired, travel-weary, and shabby. I later found out that their tour organizer had demanded additional payment for accommodation at the hotel.

It was becoming apparent that there was a massive gap between the requirements of the hundreds of pilgrims from India wanting to visit Kailash Manasa Sarovar and the resources available at each stopover place in Nepal and Tibet. All facilities needed for proper travel seemed to have been monopolized by a few tour operators, with no clarity or transparency. It was difficult to judge whether the organizers from India were in connivance with these operators or if they were just hapless victims at the mercy of opportunists.

We went to our room. After about fifteen minutes, Mamatha said, "Come on, Mona. Let's go and have our lunch."

"You go," I told her, covering my face with a pillow and turning away. I was in no mood to get up and walk a few hundred yards just for some morsels of rice and dhal.

"At this altitude, you must keep eating and drinking fluids. Please, Mona. Don't do this. Please come and have something." Mamatha was looking out for my health, so I surrendered.

In the dining hall there were about 200 guests, belonging to four or five different tour companies. Two buffet tables catered to the needs of each separate group. Guests from one travel group were not permitted to take any item from the buffet arranged for another.

There were two small tables placed separately from the buffet, containing medium-sized steel containers and a hot plastic case with *rotis* and *naans*. Mamatha and I stood in the long line holding our plates in our hands. Looking at the large groups of people waiting for food and the emptying buffets, I said to Mamatha, "I don't think there's enough food here for everyone."

Luckily, by the time our turn came, there was ample rice and naan remaining. Perhaps the small buffet planted a sense of restraint among everyone in that hall, keeping them mindful of the long line of people waiting behind them.

There were no chairs. Mamatha and I stood in a corner and ate our lunch. The food was hot and quite tasty. The mild headache I experienced in the morning had disappeared after my nap and our stroll, and after the juice and the buffet lunch, I felt a surge of newfound energy.

"Come, let us go for a walk," I said, holding Mamatha's shoulders. And we left for another adventure.

CHAPTER 13

First Look

"Mohan, we're supposed to be present in the lobby by three this afternoon for a briefing session," Mamatha reminded me as we strolled around the tidy little town of Taklakot.

By the time we arrived back, the whole group had assembled. We stood against the wall like many of the other members, waiting for Govind.

By about 3:15 p.m., Govind arrived. "Good afternoon, everyone," he said. "As you all know, I am Govind. I will be accompanying you as group leader throughout the rest of the trip. I want to say a few words about the next four days, Lake Manasa Sarovar and our trek around Mount Kailash. Please hold any questions until after I finish my briefing."

Govind smiled, looking around at everyone. "Tomorrow's activities will start with the holy dip. You can collect the lake's water to take home, perhaps pick up pebbles from the lake's banks and seek blessings for a successful Parikrama of

Mount Kailash. We will be doing Manasa Sarovar Parikrama, which is a thirty-six mile drive around Lake Manasa Sarovar. We will stop at the midpoint for the holy dip. Be aware, the lake will be very cold. If you still choose to take the dip, please be careful.

"We should complete our circular drive around the lake by noon tomorrow. Then we will have lunch and rest for a couple of hours. We'll be staying in dormitories with four to six people sharing each room. In the evening, we will carry out the Rudra Homa ritual on the northern bank of the Manasa Sarovar Lake. Those who would like to see the full moon and the mysterious lights that appear on the lake should be on the shore by four the next morning.

"During *Brahma muhurta*, an hour before dawn, people living in tents have heard splashing in the water of the Manasa Sarovar. As you know, lakes are almost motionless and devotees believe the splashing is from the movement of the Sapta Rishis, the seven sages of Indian mythology, who bathe every morning."

As I listened to Govind, I wondered if the faith and reverence a billion people put in Mount Kailash was really baseless and blind. I did not believe in such stories. I held the view that divine mysteries were not necessarily divine, but simply enigmas of our own making. I felt that people often confused the beauty and intelligence of nature for the embodiment of something holy and mythical. Again, I wondered if perhaps my views were too limited, as they were based wholly in the pigeonhole of rationalism. Perhaps I was the one with a narrow view of the cosmic working.

"If you choose to take a holy dip in Lake Manasa Sarovar," Govind warned, "You're not allowed to use soap there. So have a hot shower tonight if you prefer, although we don't recommend it, as bathing at a high altitude may cause health issues. Last year, two people became sick with a high fever from showering too much."

Several of the travelers listened to Govind with folded hands and intent faces as if they were hearing an evangelist giving a sermon. I stood with my hands in my pockets, waiting for Govind to end his briefing and wondering if Mamatha would allow me to take my Chinese vodka after the dip in the Holy Lake.

Govind said, "In my experience, I have come across three types of travelers: the first type sees the trip to Kailash as a spiritual journey. They are very religious and are here to fulfill their lifelong wish. The second type is those who are interested in nature. These members are very fit and are curious about the landscapes and habitation. The third type feels they are buying a chance to boast about having been to Mount Kailash." Govind paused for a while before continuing, "The third type causes the most problems."

I was sure that all the members except me were certain they belonged to the first category.

"We'll be leaving at around nine-thirty," Govind concluded. "And, by the way, from tomorrow onwards there will be no bathrooms, no hot water, and no toilets."

All the travelers met in the lobby promptly at 9:30 a.m. the next morning and handed over their room keys to Govind. There was no checkout or billing formalities. No staff was present at the reception. About half an hour later, the two buses started the journey to what billions considered the holiest destination on the planet.

And then it happened. Tony, the bus driver, started playing Chinese pop music that was so shrill and so loud that I felt like jumping out of the bus. I looked around at the others, but nobody else seemed affected by the noise.

"Am I the only one who's bothered by the music?" I asked Dinakar.

He was quiet.

"Why is no one complaining?" I asked again. "Isn't the loud music spoiling the experience?"

"Nobody wants to make an issue of it," he said. "Besides, no one speaks Lhasa Tibetan."

I replied in Hindi, "I don't mind swatting Tony on his head. After all, I'll be absolved and pardoned of all my sins after my holy dip this morning."

Dinakar tightened his lips and coughed to control his laughter.

I noticed that Dinakar was reading something connected with the Holy Lake and I inquired about it.

"These are some interesting facts about Rakshastal, the first lake we'll see," Dinakar replied. "Even though its water is salty, it is the source of Satluj, one of the most important rivers in India. Also, despite its preeminent position, Manasa Sarovar does not receive any water directly from Mount Kailash but Rakshastal does."

After a few minutes of silence, he said, "Mohan, do you know how Rakshastal got its name?"

I looked at Dinakar. "No, how?"

"It all started when the Demon King Ravana's headstrong mother fell ill and expressed her wish to see Kailasa, Lord Shiva. The Demon King tried to uproot the mountain and take it away to his kingdom in Lanka, but he failed. After his futile attempt, realization dawned on Ravana that Lord Shiva's might was infinite. It was upon the banks of Rakshastal that Ravana made a daily offering of one of his ten heads as a sacrifice to please Shiva. Finally, on the tenth day, Shiva was moved by his devotion and granted Ravana his wish to obtain supernatural powers."

"So that's why it's called Rakshastal, place of the demon," I said.

As Dinakar described the features of the lake, I rested my head back on my seat, closed my eyes, and wished that the squeaky female voice coming from the bus speakers would stop. As if God Almighty intervened, someone suddenly shouted from the front of the bus, "Hey! We're about five kilometers from Manasa Sarovar!" and Tony turned off the stereo.

I looked out the window and saw only brown arid land all around. I wondered how a lake could be situated in a place like this. Then it appeared: a streak of breathtaking peacock-blue water just ahead. The contrast of pure, shocking blue water in the middle of the dry Tibetan Plateau took my breath away. I stood up to get a better view, and Shashi shouted, "This isn't Manasa Sarovar. This is Rakshastal." Even if it was not the Holy Lake, the view was still spectacular.

The bus came to a halt around a bend on the mountaintop. We all got down and Govind suddenly ran toward the water. It appeared that he was in a hurry to take a leak or to throw up, but, in fact, he wished to pray to Lord Shiva from Rakshastal and to touch the lake with his hands. He probably felt that like Ravana, he would appease Lord Shiva by doing that. Nobody else followed Govind, as it is not advisable to get near Lake Rakshastal while on Kailash Manasa Sarovar Yatra. It was believed that if a pilgrim even touched the water from the lake, they might attract bad luck on their journey.

When Govind returned, we walked up the peak to view Rakshastal. It was a short climb and from the summit I gazed at the pristine blue lake and wondered if anything more beautiful existed on the planet. The landscape was mesmerizing and in the background, like a feather adorning a fedora hat, shone the conical tip of Mount Kailash.

This was my first view of Mount Kailash and as I stared at the mountain, I was flooded with a rush of divine familiarity. Throughout my life, I had seen many pictures of the Holy Peak. It was one of the world's most acclaimed holy places. On this morning there was no cloud cover and Mount Kailash looked spectacular. The crown of the mountain appeared like a magical ornament in the sky. Everyone fell silent, observing a moment of great reverence. Mr. Shetty and Dinakar started to chant mantras and Mamatha shut her eyes and prayed.

We all stood gazing at the divine scenery when suddenly Dinakar's sister Rajasri started sobbing, overwhelmed with emotion at the sight of Mount Kailash. Dinakar ran to comfort her. Mamatha was in awe and just uttered, "Magnificent."

She was right. This was indeed an image of unique magnificence, a sight to remember forever. Rakshastal Lake appeared like a distilled holy liquid, sharply contrasting with the brown landscape surrounding it. We spent about twenty minutes savoring the incredible visual feast.

After about half an hour, we got back into our buses. We drove on, but I couldn't take my eyes off Rakshastal Lake until it disappeared from my view.

A few minutes later, I suddenly heard Shashi yelling, "Here we are!"

I looked at the road ahead and gasped as I caught a glimpse of another body of water, this one a deep emerald blue. "We're here, at Manasa Sarovar," I said to myself. "The dream destination of a quarter of the planet's population."

We all shifted to the edge of our seats and strained against our seatbelts, desperate to get a view of what lay ahead. Within a few minutes, Tony slowed down and started moving toward the left. He then took the bus along a rough mud road for a few hundred meters and stopped with the engine still running.

Govind, who had been traveling with the other members of the group, entered the bus and announced, "This is one of the few spots where the Chinese government allows us to take our holy dip. Please return to the bus within an hour."

We exited the bus like eager children on a picnic. The air was electric with anticipation. We wanted to experience the sensation of the space, the energy, the vibrations in the air, and everything else around the revered Lake Manasa Sarovar.

Mamatha took some empty bottles, the rudraksha beads, and two towels from her duffle bag. Dinakar and Rajasri joined Mamatha and me as we walked together toward the lake.

Imagine a needle of bright blue water stretching across a brown arid landscape, with snow-peaked mountains in the background as far back as the eye can see. Now imagine that gods and goddesses once swam in those blue waters.

And there it was, right in front of us: the Holy Lake of Manasa Sarovar.

CHAPTER 14

A Holy Dip by an Unholy Man

Lake Manasa Sarovar is the highest freshwater lake where life exists. Located at over 13,000 feet above sea level, it is considered the epitome of holiness by both Hindus and Buddhists. The seagulls flying above and the ducks floating on the water were a complete contrast with the lake we had just left. Rakshastal was beautiful but lifeless while Manasa Sarovar was captivatingly beautiful and filled with life. The water was so tempting that even though it was quite cold, around eight degrees Celsius, a childlike eagerness came over me and I rushed toward the Holy Lake.

As I hurried, I looked around and saw that no one else was running to the water. I recalled how my brother Krishna had stopped breathing from the shock of the cold lake. I slowed down, realizing the sanctity of the occasion. I decided to conduct myself with extra sensitivity. It was good that a sense of solemnity overtook my energetic exhilaration, for it allowed me to avoid hypothermia from a sudden cold dip.

With all the piety I could gather, I slowly and carefully unzipped and unbuttoned my four layers of clothing. Then I stood for a full minute in just my underwear with my arms around my chest. As I opened my arms, an icy wind gusted past. I covered my chest again and started toward the lake. I first dipped my right toe in the water, planning to gradually sensitize my whole body. I started to wade through the lake, taking deep breaths. The ground beneath the lake was muddy and slimy and the water felt ice cold.

I was entering the spiritual bathtub of the gods where the water was like *theertha* served in temples. I felt a profound sense of holiness. As I waded into the lake and the cold water covered more of my body, my breathing quickened. I walked until the water was midway up my thighs and stood for a full minute, splashing myself. I kept breathing out through my mouth in huffs until, finally, I was ready.

I closed my eyes and took my first dip. The lake was not deep, and I had to bend over to immerse my head completely. When I lifted my face from the water, I felt a stabbing pain at the back of my head. I stood still, waiting for the pain to go away. It receded somewhat and I shook my head to get rid of the cold water dripping down my head and neck.

My body warmed up within seconds and I dunked again. The second dip did not feel as cold as the first. I immersed myself three more times. The last time, I stayed underwater for nearly five seconds. When I got up, I again felt the sudden pain at the back of my head. This time it was so severe that it felt like someone was hitting me from behind with a sledgehammer. Fortunately, the pain went away within a minute. I stood still, closed my eyes, and, without thinking, chanted the Gayathri Mantra three times.

I trudged back to the lake's shore, looking toward the divine Kailash. I felt emotional and filled with a sense of gratitude. It was as if I had been cleansed in pure energy. The entire experience felt special and vastly different from my previous visits to temples or pilgrimages. I closed my eyes and stood for a minute longer, overcome with gratitude, before a voice within me said, "Thank you."

Two swans flew overhead, and their fluttering sounded like they were clapping in approval for my newfound piety. The gentle tinkling from a group member's *ghanta* added a of divinity to the air.

Mamatha had been watching me from the bank and she called out to me. I turned around and went to her. She handed me two bottles, rudraksha beads and a few stones and said, "Please fill both the bottles with the lake's water and immerse these beads and stones in the lake."

"Mamatha, come on and take a dip. Why don't you get in?" I asked.

She shook her head. "No, Mohan. I'm scared of catching a cold or having one of my wheezing attacks."

I went back to the lake and followed Mamatha's instructions with great reverence and care. I did not want to take away any sanctity from the ritual by reverting to my rationalistic self-analysis.

Rajasri had heard Mamatha's protest about taking a dip. She came over to us and before Mamatha could react, she dragged her into the lake. In the water, Rajasri lashed a couple of mugs of water on Mamatha's body and poured a few more on her head, helping Mamatha complete the holy dip without dipping. Mamatha slowly gave in and allowed Rajasri to splash the water on her.

After drying off, changing into new clothes and combing my hair, I felt fresh and rejuvenated. I had just cleansed myself in the swimming pool of the *Devas*. I finished the packed lunch, which consisted of a sandwich and an apple. After I ate, I sat on a large boulder, trying to absorb all the divine vibes the lake had to offer.

I sat in lotus position in mindful silence with my eyes closed. I had mastered the skill of silencing the mind through focused breathing, resulting in a subsequent collapsing of the conscious mind, a state that is called *samadhi*. The sensations during this period are devoid of mental corruption and get firmed up as experiences at the deepest level. I sat like this until Mamatha came and tapped me on my shoulder, letting me know it was time to leave. For the first time during this trip, I experienced a complete shedding of my ego and a sense of self-surrender.

Suddenly I felt famished. I remembered that a few packets of Oreos I had bought in Taklakot were stowed in my backpack. On the bus, I took out the packet of cookies and munched blissfully. Soon the entire group started to climb back onto the minibus. Many of those who had dipped in the Holy Lake were convinced that they had been pardoned of all their sins.

Though I felt a sense of accomplishment after my holy dip, the look of several members, who carried themselves as though they had halos on their heads, was amusing and somewhat brought me back to my old worldly self.

Mamatha came onto the bus. She collapsed in the window seat next to me and looked over, eager for some profound reaction. "What?" I asked, working a piece of biscuit away from my gums.

"Nothing," she said, but it took only fifteen seconds before she couldn't contain herself any longer. "How was it? Wasn't it a great experience?"

Though I had had a profoundly spiritual encounter with the cosmos, I only nodded and chomped my second Oreo. But I was sure Mamatha could easily see through my act and was laughing inside at my cockiness. I held out the package of Oreos to Mamatha and she shook her head, giving me a knowing glance. As I ate my cookies and kept up a nonchalant facade, I joyfully wondered if indeed all my accumulated sins had been washed away.

The bus continued with the Parikrama. Although the driver increased the volume of the music as we drove, the noise of the lady bellowing in Chinese barely registered in my consciousness. This time I was in a strange state of divine bliss.

CHAPTER 15

The Gompa

There are several buildings near Lake Manasa Sarovar that tour organizers call lodges and which have no official names. These lodges offer the simplest of accommodations: a roof over your head and a bed. In other words, they offer the basic necessities needed to survive overnight in cold weather.

Manasa Sarovar is large, with a circumference of fifty miles. The place we stayed for the night was about ten miles from the spot where we had taken the holy dip. The building was built with stone slabs and had six dormitories of different sizes. Mamatha, Rajasri, Dinakar, Arun, Suresh and I shared one dormitory. It was a reasonably large room, clean and airy with big windows and wooden shutters. After we arrived, we settled down and took a short nap.

At 4:30 p.m. an elderly Tibetan man holding a kettle in his hand came into the room. By this time, I had gotten used to the yak tea that was so ubiquitous in Tibet. It no longer tasted "yuk" to me; in fact, I had begun to relish it. He also brought biscuits that were crisp and fresh from the dry air and the cold temperature.

Soon after our tea and biscuits, Govind looked into the dormitory. He said, "I will start the puja ritual by the bank in about twenty minutes. Several members are already ready and waiting. Please bring along your offerings."

Mamatha and I left right away and joined the group. Some people were strolling around the bank and picking up stones that resembled faces of deities. Arun and Suresh were praying, sitting in the lotus position while facing the Holy Lake. The sun was radiating reddish rays in the western sky, a colorful contrast to the blue of the water.

Neelakanta and Shashi had prepared a small fire alter. Govind joined them in front of the fire. He wore typical *purohit* attire: a white dhoti and a white *shalya* that left his chest and arms exposed. Luckily for me, Mamatha did not ask me to wear dhoti or the colored silk shalya she had brought along.

We sat down along with the other members, forming a circle. Mamatha removed from her bag the items she had brought for this important event, as well as the *Shloka* book containing the Vedic hymns of Rudra. I was amazed to see that Govind could recite the entire Rudra Strotra Ashtakam for nearly forty-five minutes without once floundering or looking at the book. Govind's chanting was accompanied by the whistling sound of the wind and I watched Mamatha as she prayed with all her heart: eyes closed, hands folded, with in the world.

Legends notwithstanding, I found it hard to humbly surrender and pray to a lake and I listened to the chants with my head bent, merely feigning devotion. In truth, I was drawing a picture of an elephant with a twig on the soft ground. In the distance, a dog was barking at the top of its lungs, spoiling the spiritual setting. By no stretch of the imagination could a barking dog have heavenly significance in my mind. Perhaps if it had been the cry of a seagull, I could have pictured the Devas calling.

Govind finished his chanting and I dropped the stick and kept my head bowed. Then we each carried out the final *poornaahuti* by pouring our ghee and honey on the fire altar and praying for successful completion of our Kailash Parikrama. The whole ritual took about an hour and made everyone very happy. I expressed my gratitude to Govind who had conducted the ceremony so effectively.

By the time we returned to the lodge, which was about 500 meters from the lake, tea and something resembling *bhajis* had been laid out on a table in front of the dormitory. As we sat sipping our tea, Mamatha pointed out a small Tibetan monastery constructed on top of a short peak which appeared to be about a mile from our camp.

"Mona, why don't we walk up to that monastery tomorrow morning?" Mamatha suggested.

"Sounds great," I said, happy Mamatha took the initiative to suggest an adventure.

Ganesh and Arun walked toward us with their teacups in their hands. They stood next to us, sipping their tea. "Arun, do you know that Mohan sings Kannada songs very well?" Ganesh asked.

"Why don't we have a music party this evening?" Arun replied.

"Mohan, sir, how about a small party tonight?" said Ganesh.

"Why not?" I was happy to have an excuse to open up the Chinese rice vodka I had bought at Taklakot. After some deliberations, we planned the party for 7:30 p.m. in the large room where the Mysore gang was staying.

During my short walk to their dormitory room, I tried to recollect a few of the Kannada-language film songs from the eighties. I had hidden the bottle of Chinese vodka in my pocket. When I arrived, eight others, including Dinakar and Prasanna, had already gathered. Arun joined us, bringing along spicy cashews and peanuts.

There were no chairs. We pushed four cots together and sat in a circle on the beds. Duffle bags were used as stools to place our condiments and bottles.

Sriram was down with diarrhea and he lay on his bed all evening. I started off the party by joking with him. "Sri," I said, "your butthole is delirious with ecstasy with all the holy places that it got a chance to witness. Its mouth is still open wide with wonder."

"I don't know, sir. I hope I can make it tomorrow."

"Don't worry," I quipped. "It will get enlightened tomorrow and shall carry out its duties. You will have enough confidence to let out a fart by tomorrow morning without worrying."

The party began. Dinakar and Ganesh sang together and then I performed a few Hindi and Kannada songs. Everyone tasted the Chinese vodka. By the time the party ended it was 9:30 p.m., half my Chinese vodka was gone, and I was half an hour late for my usual bedtime. Mamatha and I had discussed waking up to see the lights on the lake, and I was grateful that we had decided to sleep a bit longer instead.

I returned to my room to find Mamatha fast asleep. I was hungry and joined Arun and Ganesh for a late dinner of rice and dhal. After taking the usual acetazolamide pill, I went to sleep.

I awoke at around six and ventured out with my wet wipes, toothpaste, and toothbrush for my morning biological chores in the land of the sages. Surprisingly, though Manasa Sarovar is 3,000 feet higher than Hilsa, it was not nearly as dark or as cold. I chose a spot far away from our guesthouse and squatted for my discharge.

Looking upward, I saw a sky so full of stars that it felt like I was sitting under an infinite blanket printed with thousands and thousands of lights. The stars looked so big and the sky so near. The landscape was flat and I could see almost the entire sky. The view was breathtaking. When I brought my head down, there were even stars at eye level.

I finished my morning routine, and after our tea at 7:00 a.m., Mamatha and I were ready to walk to the monastery. "Mona, this climb is going to be our first physical exertion at high altitude," Mamatha said, as we approached the base of the peak.

"No, we took that walk at Taklakot. Remember? That was 14,000 feet," I corrected.

It was just the two of us walking in the beautiful setting. Chilly winds blasted our faces, but it turned out to be an unexpected romantic time and as we walked, I reached out and took Mamatha's hand.

"So this is it, huh?" I said, in a teasing manner, "the place where our gods and goddesses romanced together."

"Yeah, right. I'm sure the husbands were all as unromantic as you," Mamatha replied, trying to free her hand.

I squeezed it and softly said, "It's so beautiful out here. I never imagined this trip would be so good. Thank you."

As we reached the base, we could see a narrow trail winding all the way up to the top. The small peak was about sixty feet in height and was about a mile from our dormitory. "*Gompa*" is the Tibetan word for monastery. It had been built using the natural rocky vertical formation as support and it appeared to be carved from the cliff. At the high altitude, the effort required to climb the small peak felt similar to climbing the first 500 feet of Chamundi Hill near Mysore. However, even though the monastery was closed to visitors so early in the morning, it was worth every step since the view from the top was breathtaking.

The morning light illuminated Mount Kailash like a piece of jewelry in the showroom of the gods. We could see both Lake Manasa Sarovar and Mount Kailash. No wonder Tibetans call it, "*gangs rin-po-che,*" which means, "precious jewel of the snows." With the magnificent view before us, the cold temperature didn't bother us at all.

Dinakar and a few others had the same idea and followed us to the peak, while the rest decided to conserve their energy for the three days' Parikrama. After our summit we returned to the lodge, as we were scheduled to leave for Darchen for a day's rest and acclimatization before starting our Mount Kailash trek.

As we turned to leave the peak, I thanked Mamatha again. "I will never forget the dip in Lake Manasa Sarovar," I said. "And going around Mount Kailash will fulfill my promise to God."

"Thank you for bringing me here, Mohan," Mamatha said as we walked down.

"Thank you for manipulating me into it," I said, pushing her shoulder gently with mine as a sign of thankful accusation.

As usual, she ignored my wisecrack. I reached out and took her hand as we headed back to our hotel.

CHAPTER 16

The Man with the White Eyebrows

Darchen is a small town about thirty kilometers from Lake Manasa Sarovar. It sits at an altitude of 15,000 feet and seems to exist only to accommodate pilgrims undertaking Kailash Yatra.

We left Manasa Sarovar at around 10:00 a.m. and arrived at Darchen by noon. The small town consisted of a dozen small restaurants and several hotels, guesthouses and camping sites. There were also grocery stores and specialty shops. There wasn't much to see around Darchen. The guesthouse contained about ten rooms that were adjacent to each other. There was also a small courtyard and four shower rooms at the inside corners of the guesthouse. A layer of stagnant water pooled in front of all the rooms.

At the center of the premises there were two Indian toilets, where you had to sit on the ground and carry out the act. But the stagnant water we initially thought was wash water was, in fact, also a mixture of wash water and urine. Not everyone was using the toilets at night; some preferred to pee in front of their rooms as temperatures would sometimes fall to zero degrees. Acetazolamide tablets increased urination and in the middle of a cold night, many travelers were unable to control the urge.

Unlike in Hilsa, the rooms were clean on the inside. Six of us stayed in one room with our duffle bags filling the gaps between our beds. I had not washed after the holy dip in the lake, so I went to take a shower. I used lukewarm water from the rickety shower head and a half-used bar of soap I found lying on the wet and slimy ground of the bathroom. I made sure that I washed away a couple of layers of soap before I used it.

When I returned to my room I was shivering. Mamatha saw me and asked, "Mona, did you take a bath?" I nodded. "But Rajasri said there's no hot water."

I shrugged and replied, "It was bearable. I needed a shower badly."

"But you didn't take the toilet kit. How did you clean yourself?"

"There was a small piece of used soap lying on the bathroom floor."

"Yuck," Mamatha made a disgusted face.

"Well, you asked," I replied.

Unlike at Taklakot, I did not take a nap immediately after showering. Instead, I left for a walk around the town.

Mamatha came with me and we strolled along the main highway, which had a gradual but steady incline.

Along the way, we passed several interesting shops. One shop had pool tables, most of them with worn-out surfaces, and we stopped and played a few games of pool. They charged me twenty yuan, which was quite reasonable despite the uneven surface of the table. With great skill, I was able to pocket a few balls.

When we returned, an ambulance was parked in front of the guesthouse. Darchen was the last point before starting the Kailash trek and the first point before proceeding back to Hilsa. Any medical emergencies during the Kailash trek were brought down to Darchen and taken back to Kathmandu.

A few of our group members were gathered near the ambulance, exchanging whispers. I saw Arun talking to the ambulance driver. Mamatha ran toward the group with her usual inquisitiveness and I sauntered over to Arun. "What's the matter?" I asked.

"A twenty-four-year-old from Mumbai died in the hospital due to altitude sickness and the ambulance is here to collect the belongings of the family," said Arun. "His parents had brought him to Kailash and the unfortunate lad died in his sleep the first day of the trek."

"Oh my God," I muttered sadly. "Poor boy."

"The family flew in directly from Mumbai and started the trek without any acclimatization," added Arun.

A sudden altitude gain from almost sea level in Mumbai to over 16,000 feet at the beginning of the Kailash trek must have caused severe edema in the boy's brain.

That evening, Govind arranged for another briefing. In the aftermath of the young man's death, everyone was scared and eager to listen. By 4:45 p.m. all the members had gathered in the main lobby of the guesthouse. As soon as Govind arrived, he checked the pulse of all the women and older adults. He then started off with a declaration, "Any member not feeling well or having doubts about their physical condition, please do not undertake the trek."

Govind pointed to Nagraj, the bearded man from Bangalore. "Nagraj and his family have decided not to go on the trek. If you do choose to come, wear warm clothes at all times and never expose your heads to outside air under any circumstance. If I see anyone exposing their head, I will leave them behind at Darchen. Remember, this is a high-altitude trek that involves great effort and demands high fitness. I strongly advise those having doubts about their physical fitness to stay behind."

I felt that Govind was playing the "better be safe than be sorry" card by making everyone think the trek was more arduous than it actually was.

Govind continued, "This is a perilous trek since it involves an altitude of almost 19,000 feet with the constant threat of a sudden drop in temperature Always wear thermals and do not remove your clothes under any circumstance, even if you're sweating. Cover your head at all times. Do not remove your Balaklava anywhere, even while you're sleeping."

"I have a new pair of trekking shoes," Suresh said. "But I prefer my Nike sneakers. Can I trek with my sneakers?"

"If you're taking a horse, you can use your sneakers. But if you intend to walk, you should wear shoes meant for trekking or hiking," Govind responded. "In case you have not worn your trekking shoes before, walk a few kilometers before the Yatra begins so that the shoes expand properly and don't give you blisters."

"Where do we keep them at night?" Arun asked.

"Keep your shoes inside your sleeping bag during Yatra nights, otherwise they may freeze. Wear two pairs of socks, one woolen and the other cotton. This practice is important since it will keep your toes warm. High altitudes kill the appetite. Force yourself to eat and drink fluids frequently. If you don't have sunglasses, buy a pair tomorrow. Ultraviolet radiation is harmful to the eyes, especially at high altitude, and you don't want to get snow blindness. Also, apply sunscreen or calamine lotion on exposed parts to avoid sunburn."

I took out my Maui Jim sunglasses and wiped them against my chest.

"Finally," Govind concluded, "Keep an eye on each other during the trek."

Mr. Shetty raised his hand. "My wife is complaining of tiredness and headache. Is it necessary to complete the entire Parikrama of three days?" he asked.

"No. Those pilgrims who are not physically fit can just complete the first day of Parikrama before returning to the base camp. Day one is relatively easy on horseback and that way you will be able to see the holy north face of Kailash along with the west face and other unique places on the trail."

The one tip that really made a difference in my trek was Govind's advice that one should never stop, sit down or rest while hiking in high altitudes, as the body required more energy to warm up again than to continue moving. It was better to keep walking, even if you were just taking baby steps.

After answering several questions, Govind turned toward four women and an older man. "I'm sorry," he said, "I cannot let you come for the Kailash Kora."

Their faces fell. "We will be fine, Mr. Govind," said the man.

Nyingma, our trek leader and a veteran alpinist Sherpa, had been standing next to Govind. He shook his head and left the lobby. Govind turned to the man and said, "I'm sorry, but you have to stay in Darchen until our return."

Govind once again addressed the group, "Nyingma will personally visit every room and inspect each member of our group for a final fitness test. He will decide who can walk and who should take a pony. He will also veto those he feels are unfit to make the trek."

That evening at supper, I couldn't find any coffee powder. I was searching the beverage table when I felt a tap on my shoulder and turned around. "Here, take this," said Prabhakar Reddy, raising his heavy white eyebrows as he offered me his sachet of powder. I was overjoyed at his offer and thanked him profusely for his generosity.

Since Reddy had been so kind, I sat and talked with him for a while, asking him what compelled him to take this journey.

"I had been planning on the Kailash trip for some time," Reddy said, "but for the past three years, my plans to visit Kailash have been continuously canceled. I was determined to come this year."

"I'm happy for you that you could make it," I replied.

"Even this year, my wife was very reluctant to send me alone. I took time off work and convinced her that with my friends accompanying me, I would be all right."

"You don't want to retire?" I asked. I thought of my own life, where I had made the decision to sell all my businesses and not retain a single one of them for Rachita or Rahul. Both my children respected my decision, as they wished to have the freedom to discover themselves and to forge their own paths in life. Selling off the businesses had been incredibly freeing for me, and had allowed me to concentrate on my passions instead of the thousands of mundane details required for successful business ventures.

"Why should I?" Mr. Reddy said, somewhat angrily. "I'm only sixty-nine and I still have years to go before I think of retirement."

Reddy maintained a stern face. I looked at my watch without seeing the time and said, "Time to go to bed. Trek starts tomorrow."

I joined Mamatha in our room, which was squeezed so full of beds that there was just enough space to walk sideways between them. In just a few hours, the trek would begin.

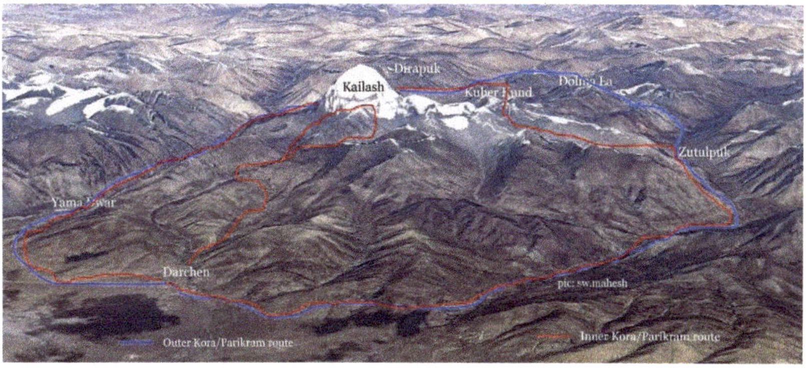

CHAPTER 17

Trekking Sticks and Horses

That evening I relaxed, lying on my bed and staring at the ceiling of our room. There was nothing else to do. The illumination from the incandescent bulb was barely enough to make out the color of the walls. As usual, Mamatha was rearranging her duffle bag. While I just rolled up my used clothes and pushed them to the bottom of my bag, Mamatha ensured that her fresh and soiled clothes did not get mixed up.

A knock on the boltless door came as a welcome respite and Govind and Nyingma entered the room.

Govind instructed, "Those of you walking all the three days around Mount Kailash, come here and stand."

Dinakar, Arun, Mamatha, and I got out of our beds and stood beside Govind. Nyingma studied each one of us from head to toe. He looked at our waists and squeezed our shoulders. He did not touch Mamatha but after taking a long look at her said in an emotionless tone, "You take the horse."

"I can walk," Mamatha protested. "I want to walk the entire trek. I've trekked many peaks in the Himalayas."

Nyingma shook his head vigorously. "*Nahi hoga* (not possible)," he said, ignoring Mamatha's pleas and leaving the room.

"Take the horse but walk," I whispered to Mamatha.

"He's doing this only because I am a woman," she said.

Mamatha went to the lobby where other members were negotiating with the horse providers. She returned after half an hour and informed me that fifteen from our group were declared fit enough to complete the forty-five kilometer (twenty-eight mile) Kora by foot and the rest of the members were instructed to take horses.

"Nyingma has not agreed to any woman trekking by foot," Mamatha said, sounding angry. "I booked a horse for all the three days along with a rider and a guide. You can take the guide since the rider will be with me."

Everyone in the room started discussing the trek. "We should try to stick together as a group so we can keep an eye on each other," Arun said.

"It won't work when some are on ponies and others are walking," Dinakar replied.

"We should make sure that nobody goes alone."

"Even that may not be possible at all times," Dinakar protested. "The stride and walking speed of each person is different. But let us not worry too much. There will be about a hundred and fifty people doing the trek and we are unlikely to be alone for long distances."

It was around 9:00 p.m. when we went to bed. The thought flashed through my mind, "Will I die from altitude sickness?" Already twelve pilgrims had died trekking that year and it was only mid-June. "Not a chance. I am fit as a fiddle," I said to myself. I spent a few minutes practicing my breathing routines and went to sleep.

Breakfast the next morning consisted of *pulkas* and *subji* and was served before we proceeded to the starting point of our trek.

"Please check your trekking sticks one more time," Govind instructed us before we entered the bus. I took out the sticks I had purchased from Amazon. These sticks had been my only contribution to the tour arrangements and were the foldable variety with three rotatable sections. I tried to adjust the height and realized in horror that the sticks were broken.

"Don't tell me they don't work," Mamatha said, as we sat down on the bus. She looked horrified. During our treks in South India, I used to tease her that she needed a stick to climb a molehill.

"What's the problem?" Neelakanta asked, seeing Mamatha struggling with the trekking poles.

"Our sticks aren't working," I explained. "Can we rent poles somewhere?"

"Yes," Neelakanta replied. "There's a shop on the main street."

Mamatha jumped out of her seat. "I remember seeing trekking poles on sale a few hundred yards from here." She hurried off the bus and ran to the nearest store, about half a mile away. She bought two sturdy trekking poles and rushed back with them in her arms. Again, Mamatha had come to my rescue.

The bus left at 10:30 a.m. We were on our way. During the next two-and-a-half days I would be hiking a distance of forty-five kilometers. I was thinking more about the fact that there would be no beds, no showers, and only rocks to use as toilets than about the fact that by completing an extremely holy ritual I would be erasing all my sins.

When the buses arrived at Tarboche, the drop point for the Mount Kailash trek, we all gathered in a clearing a few hundred meters from Yam Dwar, where we met up with the horses, guides, and porters.

The scene was reminiscent of a Hollywood movie set: the pilgrims resembled merchants from medieval times with their backpacks and small bags and horse owners held on to their animals while bargaining with their prospects. Although the Tibetan Porter Union had devised a lottery system to ensure horses would be available for all pilgrims, it did not seem to reduce any of the chaos. As we waited, the porters took a survey stroll around us, gauging and judging the members and their loads. Trekkers had come from across the globe and included a few single women, mostly Americans. There were also European couples and many Indians and Tibetans. Mamatha took the initiative of dealing with the porters and horse owners.

An elderly porter approached us, holding a hat filled with folded paper chits for our group. Each chit contained the name of a porter and his horse. Everyone picked from the hat to choose the porter who would be accompanying them. The commotion of the bargaining and negotiation process lasted for about half an hour and was utter mayhem. Mamatha asked me to wait with the backpacks and went with Nyingma. After exchanging numerous hand signals and head shakes and with some assistance from Nyingma, she struck a deal for a horse with a rider and a porter guide.

"Mohan, you take the guide and I will keep the horse rider. That way, each of us will have someone to accompany us.

"I don't need anyone. The trail seems quite wide and straight." I was keen to experience the trek in solitude.

"Listen to me, Mohan. I don't want you to go alone," she protested.

I relented more for Mamatha's peace of mind than for my desire to have a guide. But, in the end, I was glad to have someone with me.

Nyingma handed me a slip containing some words in the local Tibetan script. He shouted out, "Karma," pointing to a man standing nearby.

My guide turned out to be a tall, handsome Tibetan. He was dressed in a *chupa*, a loose-fitting robe with long sleeves and a wide waist open on the right side. The robe was made from a red woolen fabric edged with fur and colorful cloth. He wore trousers that did not even cover his ankles, short boots without socks and a felt hat.

As we did not speak a common language, we communicated only through gestures. I thumped my chest to introduce myself, saying, "Mohan."

"Karma," he responded, smiling widely.

Tibetan Sherpas are extraordinary human beings. They are known around the world for their skill in climbing the high peaks of the Himalayas and for finding safe routes for alpinists. They are incredibly strong and have extraordinary stamina. They can carry up to thirty kilos and hike up mountains with the ease of a professional sprinter taking a stroll. Sherpas routinely carry head-supported loads that exceed their body mass up and down the steep mountain footpaths. They use a *doko*, an oversized bamboo basket, which rests against their back with a strap that runs around the crown of the head. Even the women carry three duffle bags effortlessly on their backs.

The Parikrama commenced from a small *stupa*, a mound with a path for pilgrims to pass through. It was called "Yam Dwar", which meant, "the gateway of the God of death".

Yama is the Hindu lord of death, represented as traveling on a wild buffalo with a mace in his hand. Yama is believed to carry our souls when we die to adjudicating authorities, who then allot each soul to Heaven or Hell. Passing through the narrow way of Yam Dwar was supposed to guarantee a successful trek. Since both Mamatha and I had the traditional habit of going around a shine in a clockwise direction, we circled Yam Dwar three times before going through.

"Mamatha, do we proceed on the trek together or separately?" I asked as we headed out from the stupa.

"Since we both have someone with us, I don't think we need to stick together. We'll meet at the camping site in the evening,"

"Are you sure, Mamatha?" I asked.

"Yes. I will take my own time. You carry on," she said, practically pushing me away.

The weather was pleasant, with the sun shining brightly. The terrain was barren yet captivatingly beautiful. Karma offered to carry my backpack, but I declined. It only contained two pairs of undergarments and a bottle of juice that Mamatha had prepared for me.

I wondered if I should make a wish while circling the holy mountain, but I could not think of anything more to desire since my fiasco with my Bangalore property was over and I was already blessed with everything a fifty-eight-year-old man could wish. I decided instead to thank the Universe, to feel the surroundings and the ambiance during the Parikrama.

The weather was in our favor and we could see the south face of Kailash very clearly. It was eleven in the morning. I started my trek slowly and gradually picked up speed. I walked quite rapidly and often ended up ahead of everyone else. At one point, the distance between Karma and me began to rapidly increase. I looked back and saw him signaling at me to slow down by raising both his hands and lowering them, as if he were fanning me.

It dawned on me that I was in the holiest place in the Hindu tradition. Kailash Parikrama was the journey of a lifetime and I may never get the chance to come again. I decided not to rush but to explore and absorb my surroundings. There were large herds of yaks moving across the plains at a distance and the view rivaled photographs in *National Geographic*. I could only gape at the magnificence. Gradually the setting started to overwhelm me and I felt that the mountain was speaking to me.

Geographically speaking, I was trekking in the westernmost part of the Tibetan Plateau. It occupied an area of around 176,000 square miles and had an average elevation of over 14,760 feet. The Tibetan Plateau was surrounded by massive mountain ranges and had a significant effect on the Asian climate, causing the monsoon rains in India.

As I walked, immersed in thought and in the breathtaking surroundings, I saw two horses standing by the side of the trail, with an older couple and a young man resting on a large boulder ahead.

It had been just slightly more than half an hour since we started walking and I was surprised to see someone already returning. As I got closer, I recognized Shetty and his family.

I went toward them. "Is everything okay?"

"My mother is unable to breathe," Shetty's son Ramesh answered. "We're all going back."

I looked at his mother, who was breathing shallowly. She looked exhausted. I wished I could help her, but I did not know what to do. Karma offered them water, which Shetty's wife drank with great difficulty.

I said, "Why don't you take her back to Darchen and leave her with the others waiting there? You can join us and continue the trek. The organizers will take care of her."

"I don't feel like seeing Mount Kailash without my mother," Ramesh replied. "It was for her sake that we undertook the trek in the first place."

I felt sorry for them, but there was little I could do. When they once again started moving, I turned and continued on my way.

The first few kilometers felt fantastic. The trek was easy, with a gradual uphill slope gaining about 300 feet in altitude. After about two hours of hiking, I started to see the western face of Mount Kailash. Karma frequently stopped at elevated points along the trail and made me look around. The horizon was full of spectacular ranges of snow-covered mountain ridges while the trail was like a dry brown desert. I could see a considerable distance ahead and I noticed many Tibetan pilgrims clustered in groups of two and four, grouped by a similar pace of walking. These pilgrims were stopping and prostrating every few hundred feet along the route. Their dedication and devotion filled me with a profound sense of divinity.

I told myself that I was walking the same trail as the ancient sages of India. It was in these surroundings that the great Upanishads were conceived. I felt a moment of grandeur, recollecting that I was supposedly a millionth descendant of Bharadwaja, one of the seven great Sapta Rishis, and that I belonged to the Brahmin caste with the same Gotra. These ancient sages received the Vedic hymns from the cosmos within a stone's throw from where I was walking. The thought gave me goosebumps.

It was also in these surroundings where yoga, as a practice of union with the cosmos, was founded. And the first individual to practice yogic *asana* was none other than Lord Shiva.

Shiva resided on Mount Kailash and frequently meditated and danced on the surrounding Himalayan peaks. His contrasting bouts of stillness and wild dancing made all the gods curious, as gods and goddesses were not supposed to dance in ecstasy. They thought they were missing something and implored Shiva to teach them. Eventually, Shiva taught different levels of yogis, according to the level of preparedness of each pupil.

As I walked with these reflections and myths playing out in my mind, I grew more and more thrilled. Everywhere I looked, the landscape appeared divine and otherworldly. I felt pockets of devout energies. The plateau was so quiet that I could hear the fluttering of a raven taking off from a boulder ahead. Apart from my breathing, the sound of my footsteps and an occasional gust of wind, there was little else to disturb the serenity and there was no one in sight in either direction.

Every hour I took out my bottle filled with water, Tang, and oral hydrating solution and took a long gulp, thanking Mamatha for her thoughtfulness in preparing the beverage.

During the third hour, as I turned to put the bottle in my backpack, I felt a sharp burning pain in my right back muscle. I adjusted my posture by straightening my spine and flexing my shoulders, but this only increased my discomfort. Luckily, the pain was muscular and not caused from the high altitude. The only time the pain subsided was when I raised my right elbow and dropped my shoulders. Though the pain was not unbearable, it was burning, irritating, and uncomfortable. The cold weather exacerbated it.

I slowed my pace and tried different stretches: twisting, reaching, bending, and drooping. Nothing helped. Using gestures, I asked Karma to massage my back. His hands were surprisingly gentle for a man of his size and strength. Although his massage significantly reduced my back pain, it returned with a vengeance once we resumed the trek.

Breath operates without our conscious control and is, of course, vital to life. Even small shifts in mood or tension can noticeably change respiration. Concentrating on the breath has long been used as a way of calming the body and opening the mind.

I had practiced breath control for more than fifteen years and used it to ward off my frequent bouts of morning anxiety. I applied this skill to my current situation. Slowing down my pace, I raised my elbows to shoulder level while inhaling and expanding my back muscles. After a few seconds, I brought them down with a long, relaxing exhalation. I closed my eyes and concentrated on the muscle that was burning while loosening up those muscle tissues to coincide with my slow breath. After about ten continuous minutes of this exercise, the pain began to subside. I continued this deep breathing as I walked on the holy path of the ancient yogis and soon my pain had completely vanished.

CHAPTER 18

Another Deathly Start

At about 1:00 p.m. on the first day of the trek, we had covered more than eleven kilometers (seven miles) and gained about 1,000 feet in altitude. We were trekking on the highest plateau in the world, on a trail that was known as "moderately difficult." I wasn't tired or dehydrated. Now that my back pain had vanished, I was having one of the best trekking experiences of my life and the surrounding scenery kindled sensations of a kind I had not experienced before.

Suddenly it started to drizzle and soon the rain intensified into a shower. This was not the rainy season in the southwestern Himalayas and I was not prepared for a downpour. A gust of icy wind lowered the temperature drastically. Thankfully, Karma had brought me a plastic rain jacket with a hood. The rain soon lessened, but the wind remained strong. It was difficult to see the trail ahead and we were forced to slow down our pace.

Then, as suddenly as it had started, the rain stopped. I passed a small descent and I was surprised to see a lone, middle-aged Indian woman ambling ahead. I approached her and said, "Namaste."

"Namaste," she replied, clasping herself tightly against the chill wind. She stopped to pull down her balaclava. A scarf covered her mouth and nose. I could only make out her eyes and the *bindi* between them.

"Are you all right, Madam?" I asked.

She nodded.

"Do you need any help?"

The woman relaxed and said, "No, thank you. There are many Sherpas behind who are helping those who are slower than me. We were all together in the beginning, I don't know what happened to us. We went through government tests for our health—lungs, heart, everything. There were fifty-six of us when we started, but half turned around at Lake Manasa Sarovar. Two died there, one a woman of just forty. Something happened in her chest. So we began to feel afraid."

Although the woman looked like she had never climbed anything higher than the staircase in her house, I said, "I'm sure you'll be fine. Please wait and join your group." Then Karma and I continued on ahead.

At around two in the afternoon, the midpoint of the day's journey, I saw a few horses tied to wooden posts outside what appeared to be a tea shop. The shop was constructed from mud and had a tin roof. It was a relatively large place with six wooden tables that could each accommodate about six people. The tables were rugged and heavy with roughly-finished edges. Two tables were occupied by a group of Sherpas who were arguing and eating Tibetan noodles. To our left stood a cast-iron stove where cauldrons of tea were brewing slowly over smoldering yak dung.

These tea shops were set up during the pilgrimage season, from the end of April through October, and were dismantled each winter.

Karma and I entered the tea house. "Chai?" he asked me, bringing a nonexistent teacup to his mouth with his right hand.

I gave an exaggerated nod. "Just tea."

Karma pointed his finger to one of the tables and I sat down gratefully. It was warm inside and I happily removed my gloves. My legs welcomed the rest and my back muscles celebrated the welcome respite. After ordering my tea, Karma joined the table with the group of Sherpas.

The drink was served in a tall glass. The infusion was hot and murky with a mild tea flavor. It was strangely salty and after a few sips it started to taste fantastic. When my glass was empty, the elderly waiter refilled it from a thermos flask corked with a knob of wood.

Even though the place felt warm, the temperature was still in the single digits and the tea cooled down quickly. The beverage had a hydrating and energy-boosting effect on me. After my second cup, I felt some soft sediments in my mouth and I took them out to inspect them. At first they appeared like soft mud or cotton, but they were only tea dust.

Shortly after, Ganesh entered the teashop and joined me at my table. He was carrying a heavy bag loaded with emergency medicine and oxygen canisters.

"Mr. Mohan, can I use your guide to carry my backpack?" he asked. "It's heavy with the oxygen canisters."

I shrugged. "It's fine with me, but that's something only Karma can decide."

The waiter came to our table and raised the jug of salty tea toward Ganesh. Ganesh looked at him and nodded.

"I wonder how Tibetans adapted to these cold, high-altitude conditions," Ganesh pondered. "Nine of the world's fourteen highest mountains are in Tibet, and they are all higher than twenty-five thousand feet."

After twenty minutes I was ready to leave, but Karma kept chatting with his friends. I waited another ten minutes and then I tapped my watch, signaling to Karma that it was time to go. He looked at me and merely nodded. At first, being the restless soul that I am, I started to feel irritated at his indifference. Then I relaxed as I realized Karma was deliberately delaying so that I could get acclimatized to the higher altitude. I took a deep breath and remembered an orange Mamatha had taken from the buffet table and placed in my backpack. Her concern and thoughtfulness had saved me many times in the past. I gratefully removed the orange from my backpack, peeled off the skin and offered half to Karma. He shook his head.

Karma remained engrossed in conversation and I had to wait about half an hour before he was ready to leave. Then he placed the orange skin I had left in one of his bags, being careful not to litter. Ganesh exchanged hand gestures with Karma until they worked out a deal: Karma would carry Ganesh's heavy backpack until the end of the day for 200 yuan.

"Thank you, sir," Ganesh said to me, sipping his tea.

"No problem, Ganesh."

Free of the heavy bag, Ganesh stretched both his arms wide as we stepped outside. The Tibetan tea had rejuvenated us and Karma, Ganesh and I set off at a brisk pace. Though it felt cold, we were used to the temperature. I wore four layers of clothing and my first layer, a thermal shirt, was moist with sweat. The pain from my cramps had vanished entirely. The electrolytes from the salty Tibetan tea along with my deep breathing exercises had helped to relax my muscles. I moved quickly, and, despite his size, at first Ganesh kept up.

Again, the trek was breathtakingly spectacular. I stared in awe at the barren plateaus with occasional patches of green. There were narrow passes, winding streams, and, like the icing on a celestial cake, Mount Kailash with its snow-covered peak shining in the distance.

Ganesh slowly began to fall back. When he was about a hundred yards behind me, I paused to let him catch up, my chin resting on the trekking stick.

"I think it will be wise for us to take the horses tomorrow," Ganesh said. "We will have to trek fourteen miles at a high altitude. I'll be taking a pony even though I know they'll charge a bomb. What about you?"

I did not need a horse. It was the challenge of walking the entire distance at this altitude that thrilled me. I had completed many treks, but none at 19,000 feet, none in the Himalayas, and certainly none around a holy mountain.

I just said, "I will see tomorrow." After pausing for Ganesh to catch up with me several times, I carried on without waiting.

The view of Mount Kailash made me feel inspired and spiritually touched. A pure, divine feeling started to envelop me. I felt a strange mix of surrender and reverence. This feeling was spontaneous and did not evolve from my rational mind or my memory. For the first time in ages, I thought of God manifesting in these mountains. Involuntarily I chanted the Vedic *Gayatri Mantra*.

I felt a little warm, so I removed my jacket and tied the sleeves around my waist. Karma strode toward me shaking his head vigorously, displeased that I had removed my outer layer. He made frantic gestures asking me to put it back on. I conveyed with my own, equally-vigorous gestures that I would be fine, showing him the sweat that drenched my shirt.

At first, I felt cool and very comfortable. But within a few minutes, a cold gust of wind with the sound of a low-pitched whistle hit me. It felt like a splash of cold water. I almost froze. I began to shiver violently and hurried into my jacket, zipping it to the neck and covering my head with the woolen hood. I hugged myself, rubbed the tip of my nose to warm it, and carried on.

At this point, I was trekking at around 16,500 feet. The tingling sensation in my fingers and lips from the acetazolamide was not unfamiliar to me, as I had taken acetazolamide pills for elevated eye pressure several years earlier. I was feeling fit despite the sudden drop in temperature and I increased my pace, leaving behind Karma and focusing my mind on my trek. The terrain was flat and undemanding and the scenery was surreal.

At around 3:00 p.m., Karma suddenly overtook me, detouring to the right and beckoning at me to follow. He stopped on a small rise. As I walked toward him he raised his hand, pointing his index finger at something far away. I stood next to him and looked where he was pointing.

I froze, stunned by the sight of the imposing north face of the holy natural shrine. Nothing in the world could prepare someone for a view such as this. Mount Kailash stood like a mammoth granite pyramid with its north side completely visible from base to tip. It looked extraordinarily divine. I sat down, closed my eyes, and started to meditate. Then I simply sat looking at the snow-ornamented rock, fully experiencing this magnificent vision of Kailash.

After several minutes, Karma tapped my shoulder, reminding me that we still had some way to go before reaching our destination for the day. I rose, reluctant to leave the view behind, and took slow steps to join Karma. A few minutes later, I suddenly recalled the only other time I had felt so awestruck and close to God.

In 1986, I was twenty-eight years old and had just finished my quota of debauchery in Las Vegas. I booked a private tour in a small Cessna that was supposed to take me to a fascinating place close to Vegas. I had paid for the trip from my casino winnings and had no idea where I was going.

We got off the plane and followed the tour guide a few hundred yards to the spot where the attraction was situated. I looked ahead and gasped. A gigantic crack in the ground lay in front of me. The break looked about a mile deep and a mile wide. My mouth fell open with shock and wonder. For the first time in my life, as I faced the Grand Canyon, I believed that God truly existed.

At around 4:00 p.m. we approached a large bridge with prayer flags on it and I saw a monastery in the distance. It was the Dirapuk Monastery, a large red building with four yellow stupas on top and a white brick wall all around. It was situated close to Mount Kailash, with the north face of the holy mountain in the background. I remembered something Govind had said during his briefing, "Do not mistake the monastery as our camp, you must go further up toward Kailash." Our accommodation was further up in a corrugated tin building with an all-dirt floor that lay on the main trail right under the shadow of Kailash.

Karma and I soon arrived at Dirapuk camp, which was located about a mile from the monastery. It was a small, man-made clearing with a row of single-room huts with walls of dried mud and tin roofs. There were a couple of food tents nearby and several horses tied up in the stone enclosure.

Karma went into one of the huts and brought out a man who pointed at the second room. I went inside. The room contained six wooden cots and mattresses. Each cot had a thick woolen blanket folded at one end and a single bare pillow at the other. Even though it was only afternoon, the hut was damp and very cold.

I peered inside the first room and was surprised to see Akash Gowda from Mysore.

"You came now?" he said, "I came long back."

None of the members with horses had arrived and I wondered how horses could take longer than men to cover the same distance.

First, I went back to my room and slept for an hour. I was completely comfortable and at ease with the altitude and had no headache whatsoever. After I awoke, I went to the food tent and got some instant noodle soup and black salt tea in a plastic cup, still greasy from the previous diner. I took the cup outside and sat on a boulder.

By then, most of the members of our group had arrived. About fifteen had chosen to walk and many of them were talking to the horse owners about hiring horses for the next day. The horse owners spoke fluent Hindi and these opportunists took advantage of the hapless pilgrims who had chosen not to hire horses at the start of the trek, using fear to promote their services.

"The oxygen will drop and climatic conditions will be worse tomorrow," one horse owner warned. "You'll have to cross big rocks and glaciers."

"You may not get medical assistance on the way," another owner threatened. "The second day of the trek takes the lives of dozens of people each year."

Out of fifteen trekkers, only four—including me—decided to continue on foot the next day.

As I watched the horse owners in amusement, sipping my Tibetan tea, I started to wonder why Mamatha had not yet arrived. I got up, put my empty cup in a tub and asked Prasanna if he had seen Mamatha.

"I saw her walking along with her pony and her horse rider at around one in the afternoon," said Prasanna. "Why don't you ask the trek leaders?"

I went to Neelakanta who shrugged his shoulders and said, "How would I know?"

I became furious at Neelakanta's complete indifference for Mamatha's whereabouts. I stared him down until he left to ask each member if they had seen Mamatha. Geetha, who had just arrived on her pony, said that she had seen Mamatha walking near the halfway point.

Govind came out of his shack to find out what was happening. When he heard I was looking for Mamatha, he took my arm and guided me to the edge of the camp. He then pointed downhill toward the Dirapuk Monastery. He said, "Why don't you go and check there?"

I looked incredulously at Govind, wondering if he was joking. It was almost evening and the monastery was at least 700 feet downhill. I had just completed a sixteen-kilometer trek at an altitude of 16,500 feet, and Govind expected me to stroll down the mountain to check if my wife had mistakenly landed there? Besides, I spoke no Tibetan or Mandarin. It would have been more useful for one of the Sherpas with Himalayan stamina to go and inquire in their native language.

"Isn't there any other way of communicating with the monastery?" I asked with a pleading face.

Govind shook his head. His expression seemed to convey, "Well, it's your wife." Instead of speaking his mind, he merely said, "Sometimes porters mistakenly take members there and the monastery accommodates tired pilgrims doing the Kailash circumambulation. You would be helping the entire group."

The thought of helping others motivated me enough that I set out downhill. Nobody else offered to accompany me. It took over twenty minutes to travel the trail to the monastery and I worried the entire way that Mamatha had collapsed somewhere along the path. When I arrived, I was dismayed to see the many steps that led to the monastery entrance. I clambered up the stairs and by the top I was almost on my knees and hands.

The monastery contained many large dormitory-type rooms. The windows were large and offered a magnificent view of Kailash. The entire place appeared to be deserted. I wondered how such a large monastery could have no one to guard it. Finally, I spotted someone crossing the corridor and I ran after him before he could disappear. He looked like the Tibetan Lamas from the settlement at Bylaguppe, close to my hometown.

"Hello," I said. The monk stopped and looked at me. "Do you speak English?"

"*Aap Hindi jaante hein?* (do you know Hindi?)" he asked in impeccable Hindi. I felt thrilled that we could communicate.

"Is anyone from Kailash Treks here at your monastery?" I asked in Hindi.

"No. No one has come till now," the monk said.

I explained that members of Shekar Treks might mistakenly end up there and asked the monk to send them to the campsite at Dirapuk. He nodded and said, "Sure, I will."

The climb back to camp took thirty minutes and each minute seemed to last a lifetime. Every step on the stony track was a battle between my legs and my mind.

By the time I returned to Dirapuk, Mamatha had still not yet arrived. When I heard that she was still missing, I became even more worried. The thought of Mamatha in trouble began to haunt me.

A few years earlier, we had visited the Maldives for Mamatha's forty-third birthday. We had been desperate for a break and the images of the incredible beaches enticed us to go. The beauty of the Maldives lived up to its reputation, with pristine ocean water stretching for miles.

On the third day of our stay, we hired a catamaran to go out on the Indian Ocean. The strict-looking boat owner assured me that the teenage sailor he assigned us was an expert and there was no danger. Mamatha and I strapped on our life jackets and set sail. It was a windy day and as we left the shore, we made sure that our legs were firmly twined in the catamaran's ropes.

The island quickly disappeared from view and soon we were alone in the middle of the Indian Ocean. Playful dolphins interrupted the vast solitude. After about an hour of sailing, a sudden fierce gust of cold wind came sweeping by. Before the young sailor could maneuver the mast, the catamaran capsized and dumped us all into the ocean.

The force sent me plummeting twenty feet through the churning water. When I surfaced, I hung onto the rim of the capsized catamaran for dear life. I wiped my nose and eyes to expel the salty water and looked around for Mamatha. I could not see her anywhere.

"Mamatha, Mamatha," I shouted frantically as the panicked sailor swam around, searching.

The two minutes that it took for Mamatha to surface felt like a lifetime. Finally, I saw her life jacket balloon up and then Mamatha's head broke the surface. She gasped and gulped for air. Mamatha had not been able to wriggle out of the rope around her feet and her life jacket had come loose, slowing her ascent. Because of the unexpected weather change and the ineptitude of the young sailor, she had almost died.

I shivered as I remembered Mamatha's close call on the ocean. But this trek was different. On this trip, Mamatha had a horse and a local rider. I tried to reassure myself that she couldn't possibly lose her way.

Two-and-a-half hours had passed since my arrival and it was already dusk. I was worried sick and I did not know what to do. I looked around the camp, determined to take Govind by his collar and make him send a band of Sherpas in search of Mamatha.

Suddenly, I heard clapping. There was Mamatha, with her pony and porter, slowly making her way up to camp. She was safe and smiling. And as was customary in all our treks, Mamatha came steadily, crawling up to the camp like a never-failing turtle.

CHAPTER 19

A Marvel in the Mountain

At the sight of Mamatha I almost broke down. But I had been taught that it was unmanly to cry or express deep emotion so hiding my relief and exaggerating my frustration, I merely said, "What took you so long? You're the last one to arrive."

"I walked the whole way. I didn't use the horse," Mamatha replied.

With that, she turned to her rider and asked, "*Hum pedal ayena*?" (Didn't we come walking?)

The rider cocked his head and confirmed, "*Mem sahib Goda use nahikiye*." (Madam did not use the horse.)

"Wow. Well done, Mamatha." I was impressed by her stamina.

It was around 6:30 p.m., but still not dark. I showed Mamatha to our room, which was now also occupied by Arun, Suresh, Rajasri, and Dinakar.

Mamatha sat on the first single bed right near the entrance, where I had placed my backpack to reserve the space. Each bed was just wide enough to turn around and I had to crawl to my cot. Dinakar was sitting bare-chested on his bed.

"What are you doing, Dinakar?" I asked, shocked to see him half-naked in the cold.

"Govind frightened me and against my better judgment, I wore more layers than I should have and got overheated on the trek. As soon as I arrived, I started shivering uncontrollably. I realized I was beginning to feel hypothermic. My cotton base layer was drenched in sweat and I stupidly did not remove my jacket."

"But how did removing your clothes help?" I asked him, bewildered.

"I stripped down and got under the dry sheets of my bed. After a cup of hot chai, I felt much better."

Neelakanta began visiting each room to ensure the members had returned and were all right after the first day's trek. When he came in and saw Dinakar topless, Neelakanta started yelling, "Are you crazy? Haven't we told you to wear multiple layers at all times?"

"Chill, Mr. Neelakanta," Dinakar replied. "I know what I'm doing. I've done many difficult treks in Colorado."

Neelakanta shook his head and left.

It was going to be dark soon and I was keen to get as close as possible to Mount Kailash. "Mamatha and I want to sit in front of the north face for a while," I said.

"Rajasri and I will join you." Dinakar got up and put on his clothes and we started toward the foothill of the north face of Kailash. The distance was only about a few hundred yards and the terrain was flat. Kailash looked golden-brown in the late evening sky.

We sat down in the lotus position close to the foot of the mountain. Dinakar and his sister chanted the *Rudra Mantra*. I began to chant the *Mahamrityunjaya Mantra*, the ultimate mantra to free oneself from the insecurity of the constant fear of death.

"Oh, three-eyed Shiva, fragrant nurturer of life. May I be bestowed with liberation from the fear of death for the sake of immortality, as the cucumber is severed from its bondage to the creeper."

A few Tibetan Lamas walked up the steep terrain leading to Mount Kailash to touch its base. This ritual is considered extremely holy and is called *charan sparsh* by devout Hindus. Although I was exhausted, I, too, wished to take a closer view. I got up, dusted my posterior with my hands and asked Mamatha if she wished to join me.

Mamatha shook her head. I looked at Dinakar. He said, "It appears very close, but it's a six-kilometer walk up to the base from here," He explained that he did not want to push himself too much before the Dolma La pass climb the next day.

I looked at Mamatha, who was sitting on the ground alongside Rajasri. I asked again, "Mamatha, are you sure you don't want to come?"

Mamatha shook her head. "No. You go."

I started toward the holy peak, more to touch it and feel its surface than to seek its blessings. I mustered my reserves to climb another 800 feet for the charan sparsh, even though I had walked more than sixteen miles that day.

The terrain that led up to Mount Kailash was uneven and inclined upwards. There was no boundary to show precisely where Mount Kailash started since the granite formation had no clear demarcation. As I got closer, the panoramic view of Kailash appeared different. From closer up it resembled an alien carrier, stuck in the ground. I began to feel an entirely different kind of eagerness, coupled with a spiritual excitement. I was approaching a mystical natural wonder.

I moved up another few hundred feet, very close to Mount Kailash. I turned around and looked behind me. No one was there. Although I was tired, sweaty, huffing and puffing, the desire to experience more of the aura of Kailash kept me energized despite my exhaustion.

The terrain was confusing as there was no designated path on the slippery and snowy ground. All I could do was walk in the direction of the mountain. Despite the difficult trek, I finally reached what appeared to be the beginning of the base of Mount Kailash. The mountain appeared less than half a mile away, but the sky was getting darker and the granite part of the holy peak still felt distant. Only two Tibetans were returning, and no one else was walking toward Mount Kailash.

I asked one of them how far it was still. *"Abhi kitna door hein?"*

"Dho mile," he said. "Two miles." I decided not to walk any further. Going to the base of the mountain and then back to the camp could take over a full hour more, and once the sun set it would be a dark and possibly perilous walk. Instead, I sat on a nearby boulder and looked up at the mountain.

After a few minutes spent catching my breath, I noticed that it was getting darker by the minute. I suddenly realized that I was directly across from the most magnificent God-made shrine on the planet. Suddenly, I felt a strange burst of positive energy and an extraordinarily divine sensation. My eagerness doubled and transformed into an internal compulsion and a need to worship. Suddenly, I felt fully recharged and more energized than I had been all day. It was magical.

I stared intently at Mount Kailash. It certainly looked mysterious. As I gazed at the mountain, it appeared to take on different forms. First it resembled the hood of a large king cobra, carved out by Mother Nature. Next, it looked like an alien pyramid made out of some sophisticated mineral, symmetric and elegant. Finally, the holy mountain looked like Lord Shiva's abstract symbol of *linga*, representing energy and strength.

I closed my eyes and thought about my life. Flashes surfaced of the death threat from Jalli Jagdish. But now, my whole life seemed so insignificant that an embarrassed grin formed on my face. In the spiritual shelter of the towering Kailash, life and death seemed inconsequential. All my possessions and achievements appeared trivial. I marveled at the cosmic hand that had guided me to Kailash and Manasa Sarovar to show me the magnificence of the divine design.

At that moment, Mount Kailash changed for me. It went from a spectacular natural wonder to a mystical shrine. I looked at the mountain again and again. Each time, I felt fulfilled and thanked the holy mountain that had brought me here. I wanted to hold the moment forever.

Even though darkness was enveloping everything around me, I was reluctant to leave. Finally, I started back with a mind that had been cleansed and transformed and a soul that was much closer to salvation.

When I reached the camp, Mamatha was still sitting with Rajasri and Dinakar. It was fully dark outside. We returned to our rooms and rested before dinner. At 8:00 p.m. sharp, Mamatha and I left the room and headed toward a small open area that had been cleared and leveled. The surrounding area was rocky and uneven and we had to walk with care. Three long, narrow wooden tables had been placed alongside each other and local cooks had laid out metal pots containing *kichdi*, rotis and dhal. Neither one of us felt hungry, but Mamatha and I were aware that we needed to eat and hydrate well.

Standing outside in the cold night, we ate the hot but bland kichdi, a little rice, and two pulkas. I could feel the warmth of the kichdi in my stomach. After we ate, we all returned to our room to discuss the next day.

"Before leaving for the day's trek," Dinakar said, "Govind will send a few Sherpas to check everyone's physical condition."

"Tomorrow we'll see Gauri Kund, the birthplace of Lord Ganesh," added Arun. "But we have to climb Dolma peak first."

"Many have fallen sick and have decided to return to Darchen," Dinakar added.

"How many?" I asked.

"About fifteen."

"Since this is the highest-altitude camp, most usually decide to return to Darchen on this night," Arun said. "Also, Govind decided not to allow those with altitude sickness on tomorrow's trek."

I was feeling very sleepy. I did not take off my jacket and slept in my coats and trousers. The only piece of clothing I removed was my shoes. Mamatha lay beside me, tossing and turning on her narrow bed.

Just as Dinakar got up to turn out the light, we heard a knock. It was freezing outside, and Dinakar reluctantly opened the door, muttering, "Who in the world could it be?"

We were all surprised to see Prasanna, the husband of the athletic couple from Bangalore. "Hello, everyone," he said, entering our room. "Could any of you lend me three thousand yuan? I've decided to take a pony for tomorrow and I'm running short of cash. I'll pay you back as soon as we reach Taklakot."

I was surprised to hear that Prasanna wanted a horse since the couple appeared very fit. At the start of the trip, I had looked at his muscular body and his bulging biceps and had vociferously predicted in front of everyone that he would be the first to reach Dolma summit. I glanced at Mamatha. Not sensing any hint of resistance or disapproval, l took out my wallet to check how much I had. The wallet contained about 2800 yuan and Mamatha had about 3000 yuan from the 5000 yuan we had each drawn out from the ATM at Taklakot.

I gave Prasanna 2000 yuan and Mamatha parted with 1000 yuan.

"I'll return it when we get back to Taklakot," Prasanna said.

"Don't worry about it, Prasanna," I assured him. "We're happy to assist you. You can give it back after we return to Bangalore."

"Mohan, you know tomorrow is the eighteenth, right?' Mamatha asked me as soon as Prasanna had left.

"Yes. Turry's birthday," I said, and a surge of sorrow made my eyes moist. The next day was the anniversary of the day in 1989 that my eldest and late daughter Yogita was born.

CHAPTER 20

Dolma La Pass

"Jaago! Arise! Jaago, jaago!" Nyingma's shout came piercing through the Himalayas at four-thirty the next morning. It was a wake-up call for everyone. Thank God the southwestern part of the Himalayan range was not prone to avalanches. Although we all awoke at his first call, Nyingma went around shouting repeatedly in front of all the tents.

"Oh no, not so soon," Mamatha moaned. "I will use the horse today. Mona, you leave."

As Mamatha curled back up I stood, put on my headlamp, and picked up my toothbrush, toothpaste, and wet wipes for my early morning 'Himalayan project'. It was the coldest morning of my life. The three chores of face-washing, mouth-washing and bowel discharge took half an hour and I was freezing the whole time.

When I returned to the room, Mamatha was still curled up on the bed. She said, "Mohan, why don't you wait until there's at least some daylight?"

"It's a twenty-two kilometer walk today, Mamatha. I want to leave early."

"Govind was saying that there are some wonderful landscapes at the beginning of today's trek. Don't you want to take photographs?"

"My inner memories are more important to me than photos captured on a camera."

A Sherpa knocked on the door. He opened it and yelled, "*Chalo, jaldi*!" (Get going quickly.)

A bone-chilling wind was blowing when I stepped outside and I immediately started shivering. I pulled the Balaklava down so it covered my face, leaving only my eyes exposed. Then I put on my gloves and hugged myself tight. Karma came over with a hot cup of yak tea. I drank it with gratitude in my heart and quickly asked Karma for another cup. The two cups warmed me enough to start on the most arduous trek of this trip.

Akash Gowda, Dinakar, Prasad, and I were the only ones planning to trek the second day on foot. I knew I was fit. But I was fifty-eight years old and the other three were in their early forties. Was I fit enough to trek twenty-two kilometers in one day at an altitude reaching 19,000 feet? I reassured myself that I was definitely in good enough shape to walk the entire distance despite the challenging altitude.

The trail on the second day would climb steadily and as we got closer to the Dolma La pass, the climb would become very steep, after which there would be a sudden drop of 1,500 feet. We would be passing across the northeast face of Kailash and coming across *Shiva Stal*, the place of Shiva.

Some say the location marks the end of a pilgrim's past life along with all their past sins.

It was exactly 5:00 a.m. when Karma and I set out. The ambient temperature was sub-zero, the raw wind made me shiver continuously, and although I covered my face with another handkerchief, I was still thoroughly chilled.

On the first hour of the trek, we had to cross a small frozen lake. I had no idea if the ice was thick enough to bear my weight. This was the first time in my life I had walked on a frozen surface. The sheet of ice was elliptical in shape, about 200 feet long and 100 feet at its widest point. I could not fathom or gauge its depth. As we got closer, I saw a lone man walking casually across the frozen lake. Still, I waited for Karma to cross first and then carefully followed as he picked his way across the ice.

At 11:00 a.m., after walking for about seven or eight kilometers, Karma pointed to a steep ridge with a trail winding upwards. "Dolma," he said, as he led me to it. As I looked up, a sudden cold breeze brushed my cheeks. When I saw the trail, I thought Dolma La pass did not look all that intimidating. However, I could not yet see the Dolma summit.

I set out with Karma leading the way. The pass started with a gradual ascent and then the trail started to get narrower. After a couple of minutes of climbing, Karma hurried over, took my arm and pulled me to the extreme side of the trail. I saw a yak laden with baggage coming down from the opposite side. The size of the animal from up close was quite intimidating and it moved with no concern for other people on the trail. I nodded in an appreciative and thankful gesture at Karma. If it weren't for the timely intervention of my Sherpa, I would probably have been knocked down by the yak.

After an hour, we reached the starting point of the steeper part of Dolma La pass. Dolma La is the Tibetan name of goddess Parvati, wife of Lord Shiva. Tibetans claim that a person may successfully cross the pass only if the goddess bestows her grace upon them.

I climbed the first few hundred meters without heaving for air, although we were at an altitude of more than 17,000 feet. But as the climb became steeper and steeper, I started to feel the dryness in my nostrils and a need to take in more air. I deliberately inhaled deeper and deeper. The forty-five degree slope was long. It had rocks and boulders strewn all over and was covered with ice. Almost everyone crossed this pass on horseback, as that was considered safer than walking.

I barely managed to take five steps with every push forward and grabbed onto boulders to pull myself up. Efforts as small as straightening my back required a mountain of energy. When I moved my feet, it felt like they each weighed a kilo. Many oxygen canisters and used EPO syringes were discarded on the narrow path. Yak skulls and tufts of yak hair littered the trail. I had read somewhere that creatures died here by the dozen every month. It wasn't just the yaks who perished; most pilgrims who died on the trek collapsed on the Dolma La pass.

At last, the view changed from an ever-inclining uphill terrain to open blue sky. I could see the legendary summit of Dolma just a few hundred meters ahead. I looked back and saw Akash Gowda a hundred feet below me. He was slumped over, his hands on his knees, gasping for his breath. Even Karma had fallen far behind me. I did not want to stop, as I knew that the oxygen level was very low near the summit. The peak appeared to be only a few hundred feet away, but I seemed to be crawling at an ant's pace and it was still exhaustingly far.

I knew the best way to hike in this rarefied air was to take small steps at a steady pace and deep breaths with every ascent. The atmosphere was arid and breaths were obviously not as re-energizing as a deep inhalation at lower altitudes. My tread length was so short that sometimes my two feet were close to parallel. I covered only about six feet every minute.

As I neared the peak, I saw piles of clothing strewn over the horizon in all directions, offerings left by the locals to the Dorma Devi who graced this pass. Ahead of me, I watched a Tibetan pilgrim unfurl a prayer flag.

Legend ascribes the origin of the prayer flag to Gautama Buddha whose prayers were written on battle flags after King Ashoka took to the path of *ahimsa*, non-violence, after the great Kalinga war. Theses flags kindled spiritual energy, which could be a useful rejuvenator while trekking. Tibetans also placed thousands of prayer flags at the finishing points of each day's trek.

After walking for about thirty minutes, I reached the most challenging part of the incline. It was almost vertical and took me half an hour to ascend the 200 meters. The gusty winds had knocked down many boulders where flags were tied, and strings of prayer flags fluttered on the ground. The cubic rock that marked the top was barely visible behind an enormous number of prayer flags. Pilgrims had pasted money onto the rock and as they passed, they stooped under the lines of prayer flags and added a new string or two to the collection. They also chanted the Tibetan pass-crossing mantra, *Kiki so so, lhagyalo*. "Ki ki so so" invoked empowerment and happiness, while "lhagyalo" meant the gods were victorious. The pilgrims had now been reborn, their sins forgiven.

Finally, I reached the summit of Dolma La pass. I looked down on the miles and miles of Tibetan Plateau ahead. I heaved a sigh of relief and sat on a large boulder on the summit. Karma called out from behind me. He was gesturing at the path, probably reminding me to leave something behind. Pilgrims usually leave clothing, a drop of blood or a bunch of hairs as the symbolic death of a miserable life, as they believed when they reached the top of Dolma La they would be reborn again. I had not brought anything with me. I looked around and saw many pilgrims prostrate three times. I bravely followed suit, leaving behind only my ego.

Karma came and sat next to me on the same rock. He turned toward me and put his right palm against my chest, feeling my heartbeat. He then gave me the thumbs-up sign. At slightly over 18,600 feet, the altitude produced a strangely uplifting state of mind and a feeling of victorious accomplishment. Hindu sage Ramana Maharshi described it most aptly, "To go to Kailash and return is a new birth, for there, the idea of the body drops off."

As soon as I began my descent from the summit, Gauri Kund came into view. This was a tiny glacier lake in its own small, bowl-like valley. The frozen water looked like sapphires against the snow. I turned to Karma and pointed my forefinger at the frozen lake. Karma shook his head vigorously, indicating the trail was too rough to reach the water. The beautiful lake was almost mystically isolated since not a single drop of snow or ice appeared anywhere near its shores. Hindus believe that a dip in the water will wash away and expunge all *paap,* their sins and wrongdoings. But at minus-five degrees Celsius, they usually collect the ice in a container and sprinkle it on their bodies after returning home.

The descent into the valley plummeted to a steep and sudden drop of about 1,500 feet on a rocky, sandy slope. It was so steep that it became difficult to control the speed of my downward momentum and the gravity-driven acceleration made me run uncontrollably. Even the horses were galloping, and the members on horseback were forced to get off.

I felt like I had just completed a very tough marathon only to enter into another, this one a test of the knee-jerking slide. I ignored the competition. I also had to stay clear of the Tibetan pilgrims as they suddenly sat down to prostrate. I thought my trekking pole might break since the descent was almost vertical and I had to support myself on the pole for practically every step. Akash Gowda overtook me as he ran down the pass, eager to be the first to reach Zutrulpuk Monastery, the last destination of the day.

The deep faith of the Tibetan pilgrims around me was truly inspiring. Many of them used cheap leather slippers to protect their hands as they knelt to prostrate. Yet they did it continually for the forty-five days it took them to complete the circumambulation. These pilgrims were the flag bearers of Nietzsche's "One who has a why can live to bear almost any how."

For these pious pilgrims, wearing out their cheap leather slippers on the rocky paths of Mount Kailash, the 'how' was merely a minor technicality.

CHAPTER 21

Death, on Yogita's Birthday

Within minutes of descending Dolma, we came across a tea shop. It was a beautiful place to unwind after the demanding climb and exhausting altitude of the pass. I chose a table, small enough so I'd have it all to myself. Then I unzipped my jacket, stretched my arms behind the wooden bench and ordered tea.

It was around noon but I was not at all hungry, even though I had hardly eaten anything since morning. It was cold and quite sunny, and once again Karma joined a group of Sherpas who were chatting and arguing loudly. Karma pointed at me and when he saw I was watching him, he showed a thumbs-up sign, indicating that he was praising me in front of his fellow Sherpas.

Soon the tea was served. Tibetan tea is made from boiling tea butter and what tasted like rock salt. Karma joined me at my little table and ate a bowl of rice noodles and a beverage, with the unspoken agreement that I would pay for his meal. We rested for about half an hour and then I signaled to Karma by tapping on my watch that it was time to leave.

As I approached the exit, I saw Mr. Prabhakar Reddy, who had generously offered his instant coffee pouch to me a day earlier. Reddy, easily noticeable because of his thick white eyebrows, was sitting alone in a corner of the room. He had a glass in front of him. I waved at him but he seemed to be asleep. I figured that even on horseback, crossing the Dolma La pass must have been exhausting for the older man and left the place without another thought.

The trail after Dolma La pass was flat and this final section of the Lham Chu Valley to Zuthulpuk was relaxing. After walking for about an hour, everything changed. The sudden altitude drop was like magic. I felt rejuvenated, as though I had endless strength and energy, and I steadily picked up my pace.

I reached Zuthulpuk after walking for five-and-a-half hours. "I came twenty-five minutes ago, why so late?" Akash Gowda proudly asked me as I arrived.

"What to do. I am not as fast as you," I quipped.

"*Saar*, you were the first to reach Dolma summit. In truth, you were ahead of me," he said, somewhat sheepishly.

Akash and I were the only ones who had arrived and what Akash told me next equaled the exhilaration of seeing Mount Kailash's peak. It was a boon from none other than Lord Shiva for my heartfelt appreciation of his residence.

"Mohan, sir," said Akash, "beer is available here."

"Where?" I exclaimed, feeling ecstatic.

"Right next door."

The word "beer" created an ecstasy that no other name or word, Sanskrit or Greek, could have given me, especially after four days of yak tea and a grueling trek. I was aware that even though the most challenging part of our hike was over, taking alcohol could still be risky. Even the healthiest trekkers sometimes died at this altitude. But I decided that since I did not plan to lie down or sleep, I would be okay sitting erect with my beer.

"Why don't you join me, Akash?" I offered. "I'll buy you a couple of pints."

"No, sir. You go."

The hotel that sold beer was less than a hundred feet from our guesthouse. A tin placard with the word "Hotel" written in uneven letters was nailed to the front door. It was a mud construction with a large hall containing benches and tables. Two Tibetan men were talking to each other behind the counter and another man sitting on the cashier's chair nodded when I asked him, "Beer?"

"What the hell," I thought to myself. "If one must die, what better way than with a chilled mug of beer in hand. And what better place than in the abode of the Adiyogi?"

I then had the guilty pleasure of enjoying the best two bottles of beer of my entire life. Although my better half was still on a pony halfway across the Dolma La pass, I gulped my first bottle in less than a minute, as if I was afraid, she might suddenly enter and snatch it away. Then I took my time, relishing the second beer.

Two Indians, possibly from Delhi, entered the restaurant. They sat behind me and ordered a beer, hot soup, and noodles.

I was a bit relieved to see other trekkers drinking beer. As they waited for their food, they started talking loudly.

"We should have taken horses yesterday, too," one of them said.

After a brief silence, the other one replied, "I agree. We should have taken horses for all three days."

"I don't think I would have made it without the horse today."

"My friend did the trek in two thousand twelve. He told me that one of their group members turned paranoid at the end of the second day. The comfortless journey, lack of clean toilets, the high altitude, and the tough trek was too much to handle."

"What happened to him?" the second man asked.

"They heard him shouting at midnight using foul words. He was silenced by the Sherpas who forced him to rest. When they saw the man digging a hole in front of his tent early next morning, a Land Cruiser was called into the nearest possible point to take him to a hospital. He had turned insane."

I doubted the credibility of the narration and thought that probably the chap must have become temporarily delirious due to the exacting physical demands and the low oxygen. I couldn't resist inquiring about their experience, so I turned and asked the bearded man, "How has it been so far?"

"How has it been for you?" he asked in return.

I thought for a few seconds and said, "Two words: exhilarating and exhausting."

The man thought for a moment and replied, "One word: suffering." He took a long drink.

I stopped myself from bursting out laughing. "No wonder they're having a beer like me with a view of Mount Kailash," I thought, as I saw them nonchalantly and unabashedly drinking. The PowerPoint of Shekar treks and the part about "Discipline" flashed my mind.

"They're both iconoclasts like me," I thought and shook my head, laughing silently.

I finished my second beer and returned to the hotel. About ten members had reached Zutrulpuk, but no one else from the group indulged in a beer. Either they were scared to consume alcohol at a high altitude or they didn't feel it was worth the expense. I shrugged. I had had the most blissful thirty minutes of my life.

I saw Ganesh, Akash, Prasad and Arun huddled up together around Neelakanta. I approached the group and tapped Akash on his shoulder. He signaled to me to be silent and turned toward Neelakanta.

"We don't know who it is," Neelakanta was saying with a heaviness in his voice. "But it's one of the four men from Tamil Nadu."

I asked Neelakanta, "Is someone in danger from our group?"

"They're saying that one from our group has passed away from cardiac arrest."

I was shocked. A fearful silence hung between us. Then Shashi came up to us and said, "It's confirmed that it was one of the four older men from Coimbatore, the one with the white eyebrows."

I felt numb. I wanted to walk away, but I forced myself to stay with the group.

"It was Mr. Reddy, the stockbroker from Coimbatore." Shashi said, approaching us. "He was found lifeless in the tea shop after descending from Dolma summit, and he was sitting with his untouched teacup in front of him when he died."

Once again, the group fell into silence. I recalled the packet of instant coffee Mr. Reddy had offered me the evening before. And then I saw him slumped on his chair in the tea shop.

Soon, we learned the whole story: Reddy's Sherpa guide had noticed his head hanging down and his body sagging on his pony just after they had climbed Dolma. His guide pulled Reddy off the pony, slung him on his back, and ran the entire way down to the tea shop. Mr. Reddy was still alive when they reached the shop. Once in the shop, the Sherpa settled Mr. Reddy on a chair. He went to get Govind and they all tried to resuscitate Reddy. But despite their efforts, he had died.

Unbeknownst to me, I had waved at Reddy's body before leaving the tea shop, unaware that he had already taken his last breath. When I heard this, I felt a feeling of disbelief and a sense of unreality. I also felt anxious about Mamatha's welfare, as she had not yet arrived. The sudden untimely death of a member of our group was an unfortunate and shocking development.

Reddy did have a very peaceful death, and it had occurred after he fulfilled his lifelong wish of seeing the north face of Kailash. Both Hindus and Buddhists say that to die on a Kailash Yatra pilgrimage is one of the best ways to end your life. I was consoled by the thought that if Mr. Reddy could have written the script for his final exit, he would have probably chosen just this way to go. He had tried many times over the previous years to undertake the holy Kailash trek and his trips had always been canceled. It was as if his death was preordained to happen only in the abode of Lord Shiva.

Despite this, Reddy's death cast a shadow over all of us. I was shocked as Reddy's white eyebrows kept flashing in my mind. I went back to the room and anxiously waited for Mamatha's return.

At around five in the evening, the front metal door opened with a loud creaking noise. "Mohan, did you hear about Reddy?" Mamatha asked, entering the room and unzipping her jacket.

"Yes. Poor man," I said, a little startled that Mamatha had already heard about Reddy's death and relieved to see she had arrived safely from the day's trek.

"Govind told me that a jeep will be taking him to Darchen and he will be flown to Kathmandu."

"Are they taking his body to Coimbatore?"

"No. They are cremating him at Kathmandu. His son is on his way."

At dinner, there was an awkward silence among the members and no one had an appetite. And yet, everyone was aware of how vital it was to eat and drink well during high-altitude treks. We sat with our plates piled with yellow dhal and rice, knowing that eating was essential whether we slept or not that night.

I looked at Mamatha nibbling her food and a sudden surge of gratitude enveloped my mind. Mamatha had been so thoughtful toward me, adding Tang to water and placing the drink in my backpack. It not only quenched my thirst but also supplemented me with salts and Vitamin C. If not for her, I would not have completed the first two days of the trek in less than twelve hours. I was about to open my mouth to express my gratitude when Arun exclaimed, "Thank God tomorrow's trek is on flat terrain and only six kilometers long."

Everyone started talking and eating, successfully distracted from the day's tragedy.

That night in bed, I recalled the famous words of poet Kahil Gibran, "For what is it to die but to stand naked in the wind and to melt into the sun? And when the earth shall claim your limbs, then shall you truly dance."

I thought of how Mr. Reddy had realized his life's dream and how the earth had claimed him at the very top of the world. I found it extremely strange that Reddy had died on the anniversary of the day that my late daughter was born and that I was one of the very few in the group who had spoken with him.

Then, to distract myself, I scrolled through the photos I had taken during our trip. My two favorites were a shot with Karma pointing to the north face of Mount Kailash and one with Mamatha and me at Yam Dwar before setting out. Looking at what we had already accomplished filled me with such a sense of contentment that I dropped off to sleep and slept more deeply than I ever had before. Who knew that one could rest so comfortably in an all-mud refrigerator!

CHAPTER 22

Photos Snatched Away

The usual "Chai, chai" yells started promptly at 6:00 a.m., but this morning no one was in a hurry to get up. We all knew that the last day's trek was an easy jaunt of just two hours. This was my third day without a bath and my inner cotton vest had started to smell. I took it off and changed into a long-sleeved shirt over a sleeveless t-shirt. I wore the same trousers but without thermal underpants.

I rose before the next round of yells began. Finding a place to discharge my bowels was relatively easy compared to the ordeal at Dirapuk in the dark. After brushing my teeth with hot water that cooled down even before I was done, I washed my face with soap and water, surprised at the length of my scrubby beard.

I returned to the room looking fresh and clean. The yak tea had arrived and as we sat sipping tea in our room Dinakar said, "Remarkable, sir, you are very fit."

"I was always health-conscious," I explained. "Even in my early twenties, I religiously worked out three times a week. I started tennis when I turned forty-five and when I retired, I started jogging. By fifty-six, I was probably in the best shape of my life."

"Mohan, you are truly an inspiration."

"Thank you," I said sincerely. It was a huge compliment coming from such an accomplished trekker and it meant a lot to me.

After collecting our breakfast packs, we set out on our final trek. Knowing that it was only four miles, Mamatha and I set out together. I put my right arm around her shoulder.

"Now you are missing me, when the trek is nearing its end," she said, in a tone that was colder than the stream running alongside our trail.

"You were the one who went off alone with the Sherpa guide and your pony," I said in defense.

Mamatha smiled at me. She then turned to her Sherpa and said, "Please wait at the destination. I will come separately."

The last day began with an easy stroll down the Dzong-chu valley. The trail passed through a valley and alongside a stream with flocks of sheep grazing on the grassy banks. Experiencing such beauty with Mamatha felt romantic.

Mamatha said, "If this place was more travel-friendly, it would have been a great honeymoon destination."

"Yeah, right. At such a high altitude, only Samson would have the strength to take Delilah. It is beautiful, though. Hey! Look at that!" I exclaimed, pointing to yaks grazing on grassland in the distant horizon. There were prayer flags hanging above the river. The pristine rural beauty of the mountains and the plains, the waterfalls emerging from rock openings, and the streams flowing parallel to our trek route were truly surreal.

I reached into my inner jacket pocket to take out my smartphone to snap a picture. I had brought along an additional phone exclusively for my videos, photos, and notes. I looked in five different pockets but couldn't find my phone. I stopped, removed my backpack and started looking inside. The phone had everything on it: my notes, hundreds of photos and my videos. I frantically checked the pockets of my cargo pants. It wasn't there.

After several desperate headshakes and hand theatrics, Karma understood that I had lost a phone. He immediately called the guesthouse at Zutrulpuk camp. Fortunately, the network was strong and the man who answered said they would look for the phone, asking Karma to call back after fifteen minutes. When Karma promptly called them back, the man on the other end confirmed they had found nothing on my bed or anywhere else in the room.

My phone was gone. I felt devastated. I remembered that I had not left any token of gratitude at Dolma La pass. The tradition was to leave something small, representing something from your past you wished to leave behind. Mamatha, prompted by her Sherpa guide, had left money and prayer flags, but I hadn't left a token. Were my photos taken from me as an offering to the Tibetan Goddess Dolma? Or did the Universe want to make sure my memories were only stored in my mind? I consoled myself by remembering that there were quite a few snaps and videos in Mamatha's smartphone.

"How are the videos and photographs in your head, now that you have lost your Samsung?" Mamatha asked.

"My memories are fine and intact, and now I can use my imagination whenever I look back," I said, trying not to sound regretful.

"Yes, right. After we go home, you'll ask me if I happen to have a photo of that place or this place."

We sat together on a boulder and watched the river below. The sun was shining and the weather was good. We had magnificent views of Lake Manasa Sarovar in the distance and the soaring mountain, Gurla Mandhata, rising behind it. After several lazy minutes, we got up and continued our trek.

Soon the weather grew considerably warmer. It was an easy trek on a flat terrain, but for our tired legs, the route and the distance were still challenging. Some members who had taken horses during the Dolma trek joined us, walking the final phase at a brisk pace.

At midday, we passed through a small Tibetan village, which appeared deserted. In Tibet, there are often rural communities near monasteries, and pastoral Tibetan nomads live in tents. Tibetan buildings are often built on the southward-facing slope of a mountain. Most rural Tibetans live in small agricultural villages scattered around the mountain valleys. These are community clusters of fewer than a dozen houses, surrounded by fields. Many of these villages have never seen a television, an airplane, or a foreigner.

As we approached the lower plateaus, I turned around and looked back at the peaks we had recently descended. Both Mamatha and I had a feeling of accomplishment and achievement. The view of Mount Kailash on the right, a river on the left, clouds circling above our heads and the valleys below was unforgettable.

Karma clapped his hands for our attention and came hurrying toward us. He pointed to the fourth and last face of Mount Kailash, the eastern face. Since the weather was clear it was visible and any adjective to describe the view would be a disgrace to reality.

From the Zutrulpuk Monastery, the trail closely followed the river for an hour or so and then it climbed above the riverbank. There were several holes about the size of a fist gouged into the cliff walls. These were made by Tibetan pilgrims, who were always looking for stones to take home.

The trail started inclining upwards and began to segue into a narrow path with a deep slope on both sides. The trail was more like a ledge and the cliff to our left had a thousand-foot vertical drop. To our right, Arun had suddenly stopped in his tracks. He looked petrified at the sight of the steep fall beside the narrow pass. He slowly slumped down with an attack of vertigo. I looked behind to see him practically crawling the short distance of about 1000 feet over the ledge. Mamatha looked at me and held my arm.

Soon after, the trail became normal and flat. Karma pointed at a small peak ahead of us and turned a nonexistent steering wheel with his hands, indicating that after passing this peak there would be vehicles to take us to Darchen.

We soon descended from the peak and came across a small tea shop. About a dozen plastic chairs had been arranged in front of the shop. Karma, Mamatha, Arun, and I sat down and waited for all the members to join us. Karma raised his palm and showed a thumbs-up sign to Mamatha, complimenting my stamina. Mamatha just smiled. For me, it was the greatest compliment I had ever received. I felt as though I had been given a cardiac certificate by the greatest fitness fraternity in the world, the Sherpas.

I wanted to thank Karma with all my heart for his silent and morale-boosting company but found it difficult to communicate my gratitude. I stood, bowed my upper body and clasped his right hand in both of mine, shaking it vigorously. "Thank you," I said, meaning it from the very bottom of my heart.

Karma understood my message for he bowed his head. Then he smiled so broadly that his eyes squeezed shut. I tipped him an extra 250 yuan and then I waved goodbye and joined my group on the bus.

As the bus started moving, I felt a mild elation at my successful completion of the Parikrama. I smiled, recalling my initial indifference to the Kailash trip. The entire journey had turned out to be the best thing that happened in my life. No other trip had the spiritual intensity, the soul-stirring introspection, the diversity, the challenge, and the beauty that I encountered on this trek. I had never before experienced a positive spiritual energy with as much intensity in any temple or near any shrine as I felt in Tibet.

Lake Manasa Sarovar and Mount Kailash had moved me deeply and led me to discover a pious part of me that I had not known existed. These were also, hands-down, the most impressive sights I had ever seen. The sheer positive energy stirred the innermost depths of each visitor, religious-minded or not, cleansing their souls. It was truly a hidden world for the few people blessed to experience a new spiritual dimension.

I looked around at the others on the bus and noticed the glow on everyone's faces. Soon we would leave Hilsa and part from each other. I realized the trip had brought so much unexpected change in me. I had developed a sense of collaboration with my group members and learned that dedication and confidence could make even the weak and frail achieve everything they desired. People died during this trip and that was painful for all of us. But those who came back alive were fortunate, enlightened, and unique.

Mount Kailash and Lake Manasa Sarovar are places that dissolve your ego and make you realize the triviality of worldly comforts and wants. My one regret was that I did not take a photograph of Karma with my other phone. Thankfully I still had dozens of photographs documenting the trek, but not one of Karma. However, the unforgettable images I had seen, particularly the one of Karma with his finger pointed at the four faces of Mount Kailash, will remain forever in my memory.

CHAPTER 23

Contemplations

I awoke when I felt a nudge on my shoulder. The cozy warmth of the bus and the comfortable seat had made me doze off. I opened my heavy eyelids to see Prasanna, the athletic young Bangalorian, looking at me. I smiled and said, "Hello."

Prasanna reached into his jacket pocket and took out a bundle of currency notes. "Thanks a bunch for your timely help," he said, handing me the yuan he had borrowed at Dirapuk. I thanked him, delighted I had helped Prasanna successfully complete his trek.

It took about an hour for the bus to drive us back to Hilsa. The customs and immigration formalities were minimal. We walked back on the same suspension bridge to the Kailash guesthouse we had used a week before. By around 11:00 a.m. we were all gathered in a room waiting for the arrival of our breakfast and then for the helicopters to start their rounds.

"Mohan, sir, have you tried the *parathas* at Moon's restaurant right across the road?" Ganesh asked.

I shook my head. After having eaten nothing other than dal bhat, a combination of steamed rice and a cooked lentil soup, I was dying for the taste of anything even remotely Indian.

"Why don't you join me?" he asked. I looked at Mamatha and she stood up, signaling her affirmation.

The small eatery was owned and run by Moon, the daughter of the deceased founder. Moon was a young woman in her twenties who had lived in my hometown of Mysore while pursuing a diploma course in palliative care. The entrance to the restaurant was so low, I had to duck down almost fully to enter. The room was neat and tidy, furnished with benches that were both seats and tables. They were joined together and covered with long, colorful cloths that formed a kind of platform where six customers could squat, hold their plates in their hands and dine.

This was the best meal of the entire trip. The smell of smoky yak butter filled the air as Moon served parathas on plates streaked with oil stains from previous customers. She prepared hot aloo parathas and served them with yak butter and pickles. The yak butter was better than the best European butter I had ever tasted. I felt like a fool for not discovering this place when we were stranded in Hilsa for an entire day.

After lunch, we returned to the guesthouse and waited for the helicopters to return to Simikot from Hilsa. From Simikot we would to fly back to Nepalgunj.

"I feel so accomplished, happy, and holy after the Kailash Parikrama," said Arun gently, shaking his head sideways as a non-verbal swearing of his feelings.

Dinakar looked at him and then turned to me. "What about you, Mohan?" he asked.

"Well, at first I saw the trip as an adventure trek and an opportunity to test my endurance. But it turned out to be a spirit-kindling pilgrimage."

"In what way, Mohan?" Arun asked.

"Every other difficult trek made me feel larger after completion. But this trek made me feel insignificantly small in the sense that the setting was overwhelming and made me realize that I was not even a speck in the cosmic order of things. My notion of pilgrimages—temples and bells, prayers and priests—was completely razed since here there was no temple, no shrine, and no facilities. The only house of worship was the Kailash Mountain, built by the Universe itself. My epiphany, if you can call it that, was the realization of how important it is for a human being to periodically let go of all attachments, especially material ones."

"And you, Mr. Dinakar?" Arun asked.

"This trip and the trek, in particular, were truly transformative for me," said Dinakar.

"How did they transform you?" I asked.

"It put my world in an entirely different perspective. Tibetans live in what I considered unlivable conditions. They walk everywhere and yaks are the only means of transportation. And yet, they're happy and healthy."

"Something that truly lifted me," Arun said, "was the devotion and reverence placed by the four religions on this magnificent Kailash peak." Everyone nodded in exaggerated approval.

Dinakar said, "As soon as I saw Mount Kailash, I felt a strange emotion. I was in tears without realizing why. In hindsight, I can't explain what I felt. It was like a new connection with my heart. I tried to fathom what that meant, but I could not. It remains a mystery to me."

Everyone fell silent for several minutes, contemplating their holy sojourn. Then Arun said, "You know, Mount Kailash is the ultimate pilgrimage for the few chosen ones. At times, I was utterly amazed. I felt as if time froze. It was difficult to pull myself away. The holy mountain touched the recesses of my very being."

"It was really a once-in-a-lifetime experience," Mamatha added, smiling. "It was like I saw Heaven on Earth."

CHAPTER 24

Only Lucknow On

As we waited for the helicopters, I sat gazing at the river, recalling my amazement at the north face of the holy peak and contemplating my feelings about the adventure we had just taken. Were the trip, the struggles and the physical demand worth it?

Well, from a purely comfort and entertainment perspective, I can easily say, "no." We could have found plenty of other destinations for our sensory pleasures and luxurious amenities for much less money. But from the standpoint of experience, it was the most profound and actualizing week of my life. I fulfilled my childhood dream of seeing Everest. Then I proved my fitness when I completed the trek through Dolma La pass and around Mount Kailash on foot.

Although the trip wasn't exactly fun, it was, for me, the most significant adventure I had ever had. Adventures aren't necessarily meant to be fun, particularly those at 19,000 feet in temperatures of less than five degrees Celsius.

I stood still for a few minutes, wanting to fully experience every second left in the Himalayas. Then I started to comb the riverbank for a stone or pebble that resembled a Shiva linga, the symbolic figure of Lord Shiva. I found a small black oval stone with three parallel white lines. Mr. Shetty was amazed by its resemblance to an actual linga, and I gave the stone to him. I wanted him to have something special, as his family had turned back after only covering a kilometer of the trek.

Mr. Shetty was pleased with my gift, but said with a hint of sadness, "The whole trip turned out to be one big fruitless effort for us. We didn't even see one face of Mount Kailash."

My heart went out to his family and what I said came spontaneously, "You are such good people that Lord Shiva decided that there was no need for you to risk your precious lives by trekking for three days. Instead, he chose to send you back safely."

Rajasri liked my consolatory remark so much that she said, "Mohan's way of looking at it is so divinely reassuring."

After a few hours of waiting, we were taken back to Simikot by helicopter. This time I took a seat next to the window as I wanted to see the Himalayan landscape. As soon as we landed at Simikot, Neelakanta was ready with boarding passes to fly to Nepalgunj on Buddha Air, and we were pleasantly surprised at his efficiency. Unfortunately, the visibility was poor and it took another two hours for our flight to take off.

The travel arrangements from Nepalgunj to Lucknow left a lot to be desired. If I went along with the group, we would have to wait at Nepalgunj airport for several hours for our bus to Lucknow. We had not bathed in four days and I wanted a shower more than anything.

I suggested to Arun that we team up and arrange for a taxi to take us from Nepalgunj to Lucknow, splitting the cost. Arun, too, was worried that he might end up getting stranded at the Lucknow airport for hours if we did not plan alternative transportation and agreed to my idea of taking a private vehicle. He called his travel agent in Mysore and instructed him to arrange for a Toyota Innova to pick us up from Nepalgunj airport and drop us off at Lucknow. He made it clear that Nepalgunj was in Nepal and Lucknow was in India and that a vehicle with an international permit was required.

On my part, I made arrangements at a five-star hotel in Lucknow. Mamatha and I wished to stay there for a couple of days as neither of us had seen it before. We informed Govind of our plan and he was hesitant, but we were certain we were doing the right thing.

We reached Nepalgunj at around 3:00 p.m. and were met with the usual chaos. As soon as we retrieved our bags, the three of us ran outside to look for our taxi. A young driver received us and ushered us to his Mahindra Scorpio SUV. We dumped our bags into the van and went back to the airport to bid farewell to our newfound friends.

After wishing everyone good luck we departed for Lucknow right away. My entire body was sticky with four days of Himalayan dust and sweat and I was desperate for a hot shower. The thought of spending another six hours driving on the hot and dusty Uttar Pradesh roads was very unpleasant and I tried not to think about it.

We crossed the Nepalese border without any issues and stopped at a decent-looking restaurant in a small town. It is incredible how tasty tandoori roti and curries are in Northern India, and the paneer in paneer mutter just melted in my mouth. After a week of rice, dhal, and poories, I relished the meal.

To me, Lucknow resembled old Hyderabad. The monuments, the mosques and the people on the streets with *burquas* and white caps were just like in Hyderabad. The city was a lot cleaner than I expected and I was happy to be staying at the five-star Hotel Clarks.

The room looked refreshingly clean and was so luxurious after our recent stays at ramshackle places. I couldn't wait to take a shower. As the hot water splashed down on me, I felt like a new sensation was piercing my body and it took a while for me to adjust to the feeling of water rushing down my skin. I was sure that the dirt coming off me was enough to choke the drain.

Before I shaved, I carefully examined my beard and felt that, indeed, it was unusually thick for just eight days of growth. After my thirty-minute shower and a clean set of clothes, I felt as fresh as a daisy. Both Mamatha and I were dying to lie on a soft, clean mattress, and after we had both washed, we went to sleep right away.

Mamatha and I each had one particular item we wanted from Lucknow. She wanted to buy a Chikan dress, and I wanted to eat authentic *Lucknowi mutton biryani*, a dish where meat and rice are cooked separately and then layered and cooked again together.

We went to the most popular shop in Lucknow for Mamatha's dress. As Mamatha started browsing through the exquisite Chikan outfits, I asked for a stool and sat down.

"I'm returning from a weeklong trip to the Himalayas," Mamatha said to the middle-aged salesman, who was removing dresses from the racks to show her. "I'm looking for something very soft and comfortable."

"Where did you go, Madam?" he asked Mamatha.

"Manasa Sarovar and Mount Kailash. My husband completed the Kailash Parikrama by foot."

It was as if I were a celebrity. The salesman came toward me and removed his slippers. He came toward me and asked for my two hands. I held them out and he clasped my hands tightly. Then he bowed and gently brought both my hands to his eyes, caressing them.

"Is he buttering our egos to sell more dresses?" I asked Mamatha in our mother tongue. Mamatha shook her head with a warning signal in her eyes, instructing me to keep quiet.

The salesman shouted out in Hindi, "This couple has completed Kailash Parikrama!"

Four other men came to shake my hands. The middle-aged salesman said, "Sir, how many in this world have the fortune of completing Kailash Parikrama, much less on foot? You two are indeed special."

Only then did I fully comprehend the reverence placed on the Kailash Parikrama, particularly in Uttar Pradesh, the cradle of our Hindu culture.

Mamatha opened her handbag and said, "Here, please take *Prasadam*, the offerings from the Rudra Homa that we carried out on the bank of Manasa Sarovar."

The men were delighted and accepted them with humility and respect.

It is believed that people who visit Kailash change—they begin to realize who they really are. World outlook and perception of the environment as well as the system of values—they are all altered. Vibrations of Kailash have an effect on human brains, extending the range of received electromagnetic frequencies, and activating latent structures of the brain through which we can perceive the new reality.

Physically, I discovered much about myself, my capability to adjust, my body and most importantly trekking at high altitudes. I felt a huge sense of accomplishment after reaching the summit of Dolma La pass, and being one of the only four members to have walked the entire twenty-eight miles was an additional gratification. And I fulfilled my childhood dream of seeing Everest from close quarters

But my journey within was also remarkable; the lessons I learned are indelibly printed in every cell in my being. The majestic Kailash truly humbled me and made me realize that in God's plans, we humans are not as significant as we think. I, for one, was cut down to size and shown how minuscule I am! For the first time in my adult life I surrendered to a higher intelligence, shedding every ounce of my ego.

The Kailash Yatra enhanced my understanding and my awe at the greatness of our ancient Rishis. It allowed me to better understand the workings of the Universe, the impermanence of our existence as humans, the dying and the dead. Something that started out as a sheer physical challenge turned out to be the most magnificent spiritual journey.

Mount Kailash is an inner journey as much as it is a pilgrimage and a physical trek in the Himalayas. A soul connection occurs when you go there, whether you travel as a pilgrim, a trekker, or a tourist. The Parikrama is a singular opportunity to recognize and connect with the cosmic energies.

This inner reflection comes from the depths of your soul and not just from your mind. The awakening will come in glimpses from within, and your life will never be the same.

I will certainly go again.

GLOSSARY

Aap Hindi jaante hein:	"Do you know Hindi?"
Abhi kitna door hein:	"How far is it?"
Adiyogi:	The first Yogi and another name for Lord Shiva
Ahimsae:	Nonviolence
Aloo bhaji:	Spiced potato and vegetables, often served with rotis
Aloo parathas:	Wheat-based Indian bread with spiced potato
Asana:	Yoga posture
Avial:	A thick mixture of vegetables and coconut
Bhajis:	Spiced vegetable curry
Bhajjis:	Fried Indian snacks
Bharadwaja:	One of the seven Rishis from ancient India
Bindi:	A decorative mark worn in the middle of the forehead by Hindu women

Brahma Muhurta:	An auspicious time for all practices of yoga, meditation or worship. It is a period (muhurta) 1 hour and 36 minutes before sunrise
Brahmari Pranayama:	Humming Bee Breath, a calming breathing practice
Brahmins:	A person belonging to a Hindu Indian caste, Brahman
Chalo, jaldi:	"Move it, Move it"
Charan sparsh:	"Charan" means "feet" and "Sparsh" means "to touch". It is a Hindu tradition to touch the feet of our parents, teachers, and elders
Dal bhat:	A traditional meal from the Indian subcontinent, consisting of steamed rice and a cooked lentil soup
Darshan:	"Auspicious sight" of a holy person
Devas:	Divine beings from Vedic period
Dhoti:	A long cotton or silk loincloth worn by men in India
Doko	A Tibetan bamboo basket, carried on the back
Dorma Devi:	The Tibetan name of Goddess Parvati, wife of Lord Shiva, believed to be residing at Mount Kailash
Dosa:	A thin pancake or crepe, originating from South India, made from a fermented batter predominantly consisting of lentils and rice

Ganesha puja:	A Hindu ritual celebrating the arrival of God Ganesh to earth from Mount Kailas with his mother Goddess Parvati. The festival is marked with the installation of Ganesh clay idols in homes
Gangs rin-po-che:	"The Precious Snow Mountain" in Tibetan
Ghee:	Clarified butter made from cow milk used in Indian cuisine
Gotra:	Gotra refers to the seven lineage segments of the Hindu Brahmans (priests), who trace their derivation from seven ancient seers: Atri, Bharadvaja, Bhrigu, Gotama, Kashyapa, Vasishtha, and Vishvamitra
Homas:	A fire ritual performed on special occasions by Hindus
Homakunadam:	A fire altar prepared for the Homa ritual
Jain Tirthankara:	An extremely holy person in Jainism. According to Jainism, a Tirthankara is an individual who has conquered the saṃsāra, the cycle of death and rebirth, and made a path for others to follow
Jaago:	"Wake up" in Hindi
Kailash yatra:	Mount Kailash pilgrimage

Kalinga war:	A war between Mauryan king Ashoka and Kalinga territory
Kannada:	One of the fourteen major languages of India, spoken in the state of Karnataka
Kapal Batti:	A Pranayama breathing technique
Karpoor:	Camphor
Kichdi:	A steam-cooked mixture of rice and lentil with spices
Kiki so so:	Chanted when Tibetans pass through valleys. Literally meaning, "Victory to Gods"
Kora:	Tibetan word for "circumnavigation"
Lalita Sahasrana-ma:	A Hindu chant of thousand names of the Hindu mother goddess Lalita
Linga:	An abstract representation of Lord Shiva, an idol
Lucknowi mutton biryani:	A rice preparation made with mutton that is unique in Lucknow
Mahamrityunjaya Mantra	A mantra of Rig Veda recited in glory of Lord Shiva
Mukhi:	Face
Naadi Shodhana:	Alternative nostril breathing technique
Naan:	An Indian bread made from flour

Nahi hoga:	"Not Possible" in Hindi
Namaskara/Namaskara saar	A chanted verse, beneficial for mental, emotional, and physical health
Namaste:	"Hello"
Om Nama Shivaya:	A chant of reverence to Lord Shiva
Paap:	"Sin" in Sanskrit
Parathas:	An Indian bread made from whole-wheat flour
Parikrama:	Circumambulation, going around a holy place in clockwise direction
Pooja:	"Prayer" in Sanskrit
Poori:	A deep-fried wheat flour dish
Poornaahuti:	Concluding part of a Homa ritual
Pranayama:	A set of breathing exercises in Yoga
Pranic:	The vital energy in the body
Prasadam:	Food that is offered to the deity or idol in the holy place
Pulkas:	Flat breads made from wheat flour
Purohit:	"Priest" in Sanskrit
Rishis:	Vedic sages or saints

Rudra Mantra/ Strotra Ashtakam:	A chant to recite to appease Lord Shiva
Rudraksha beads:	Seeds that are used as prayer beads in Hinduism and which are produced by several species of large evergreen trees
Roti:	An Indian bread made from wheat and prepared in a tandoor, a large earthen pot
Saar:	Indian way of saying "Sir"
Samadhi:	A state of intense concentration achieved through meditation. In yoga this is regarded as the final stage, at which union with the divine is reached
Sapta Rishis:	The seven great sages of Vedic times
Shalya:	A thin silk shawl
Shiva lingam:	An abstract representation of Lord Shiva, an idol
Shiva Stal:	Place where Lord Shiva resides
Shivpuranas:	The Shiva Puranas is one of eighteen Purana genres of Sanskrit language
Shlokas:	A Sanskrit verse or hymn of praise

Stupa:	A commemorative semi-hemispherical monument that houses relics
Subji:	A spicy dry vegetable preparation
Svaha:	In Hinduism and Buddhism, svāhā is an interjection indicating the end of the mantra
Swarga Loka:	"Heaven" in Sanskrit
Theertha:	Holy water served in Temples.
Tilak:	A decorative mark on the forehead of Hindus, worn by both women and men
Ujjayi:	A pranayama breathing technique
Upanishads:	The philosophical-religious texts of Hinduism
Vedic:	Belonging to the period of Vedas, 1500 B.C.
Yajnas:	Fire rituals of sacrifice
Yama:	Hindu god of death
Yatra:	Pilgrimage
Yoga Nidra:	Yogic sleep; a systematic practice of moving awareness from our external world to the inner world